jody maroni's

# sausage

## kingdom

### cookbook

Boudin,
kishka, chorizo,
bratwurst, linguisa.
In every culture, sausage asserts itself.
—Jody Maroni

# jody maroni's
# sausage
## kingdom
cookbook

BY BRIGIT LÉGÈRE BINNS

UNIVERSE

## Acknowledgments

Thanks are due to my agents Eric and Maureen Lasher, for push, push, pushing this project through to completion; Lily Faire Binns-Berkey provided enthusiastic and unflappable assistance during the food photography—we could not have done it without her; Sandy Gilbert at Universe has capably guided the ship to its destination; many thanks to Michael Jackson for his treatise on the complex new world of beer, a world with which I am not as familiar as I'd like to be. Jackson, the author of *Michael Jackson's Beer Companion*, is "the world's leading authority on beer." He is also known for the Discovery/PBS series *The Beer Hunter*.

I'm grateful, as always, to the usual gang of tasters and especially to my splendid Greg, for never, ever saying "What. . . sausage *again*?" Thanks to Marc Freidus, for testing the cassoulet, and to Chuck Lehman for his help on the Po'Boy.

Finally, thanks to Jody Maroni himself for making such great sausages for me to work with, and last and most of all to Rich Leivenberg, for his infectious enthusiasm, sausage-oriented humor, and for always "being there for me."

—B. Binns

First published in the United States of America
in 1997 by UNIVERSE PUBLISHING
A Division of Rizzoli International Publications, Inc.
300 Park Avenue South, New York, NY 10010

97 98 99 00 01/10 9 8 7 6 5 4 3 2 1

Library of Congress Catalog Card Number: 97-61193

Archival photography © FPG International Corp.: Herb Schwartz (5), Danilo Nardi (12), Gordon Delisle (15), FPG International (17), Jacques Benbassat (18), FPG International (26), John Gajda (37), L. Willinger (45), FPG International (92).

Printed in Singapore

illustrations
ESTHER WATSON

art direction
PETER YATES

food
photography
TERRY DOYLE

# contents

**8** Notes from Brigit Binns and Jody Maroni

**10** Introduction—An Entrée in a Casing

**11** *Important Information on Cooking with Today's Lower-fat Sausages*

## PART I: THE SAUSAGE STANDS ALO[NE]

**14** A Step-by-Step Guide to Grilling Sausages

**16** Other Ways to Cook a World Famous Sausage All by Itself

**18** *Pairing Beer with Sausage, by Michael Jackson*

**19** The Jody Maroni Sausage Sandwich

## PART II: CLASSIC SAUSAGE PARTNERS

**20** Hot Potatoes, Cold Potatoes

**26** *July 4th: The High Holy Day of Summer and Sausages*

**28** Beans and Grains

**38** Salsas and Relishes

## PART III: COOKING WITH SAUSAGES

**46** Appetizers and Egg Dishes

**58** A Soup, Salads, and Sandwiches

**68** Pastas, Pizza, and Calzone

**78** One-Pot Meals and Everything Else

**92** PART IV: MAKING YOUR OWN

**95** Index

# Notes from Brigit . . . .

It's been a great pleasure for me to write this cookbook because eating and cooking with sausages are activities very close to my heart. It's what I do when I'm *not* working. Because I spend so much time thinking, writing about, and cooking complex dishes with expensive ingredients and artistic presentations, what I yearn for these days is simple, honest food.

I've always been a sausage lover. I'm not ashamed of my continuing love affair with haut dogs, but I'll admit to some health concerns. Imagine my delight when, returning to California after a twenty-year absence, I discovered a new breed of sausagemaker called Jody Maroni hawking his wares (twenty-six varieties of gourmet, low-fat sausages) not two miles from my new home. My first act after signing the lease and setting up the barbecue was to have a Sunday cookout featuring seven of the different varieties. I faxed the product list to my stranded gourmet buddies from Gibraltar to Bolivia, so they could envy me. I began to stock my freezer for emergencies.

What I love about Jody Maroni sausages is the lack of chemicals and the relatively low fat content. A sausage with no added fat at all wouldn't taste very good, but he's found a good balance; only the absolute minimum of fat to keep it moist, and then he adds reduced stocks for even more body and flavor. Not only that, but the combinations of herbs, spices, wines, and other great ingredients mean that these sausages really qualify as gourmet food. So it's a vice I can afford to keep.

Cooking with sausages doesn't have to be heavy, like many traditional Italian and British dishes that feature sausage. It's been easy for me to create light, simple dishes that are long on flavor, short on fat, and as modern as today.

Most of us who cherish a sausage or a juicy steak on a regular basis are still concerned about our health, but there is no reason why sausage should be considered unhealthy anymore. Jody Maroni and some other gourmet sausagemakers are now providing us with a food which is both satisfying, non-threatening, and virtually guilt-free. As Jody Maroni has said, "It's gourmet food for the common man."

**—Brigit Binns**

# . . . . and Jody

Sausage, in all its forms and flavors, is a supremely festive food—think about the feasts, blasts, and BBQs. It can enrich, exult, and shout down tamer fare. Sausage—simmering in its own juices and bursting with flavor—is the very definition of temptation and satiation.

I have tried to carry forward the flavorings of traditional sausage—from Bratwurst and Calabrese to Chaurice—into the newer and healthier kitchen. With the finest ingredients, today's low-fat sausage can provide the punch without the panic. Just show a little self-control. My sausages have been used by hotel chefs and fine restaurants for years and have helped spread the gospel of the healthy, yet delicious, new sausage. This collection of recipes will help you to cook creatively with sausage in your own kitchen or backyard.

I should first thank my dad for teaching me about sausage in his butcher shop. Thanks to my innumerable "tasters" in Venice and at CityWalk. Thanks also go to Brigit Binns for this book. Not only can she cook and write recipes with meticulous care and exact measures, she also loves sausage and all its uses. Brigit has been a joy to work with.

**—Jody Maroni, Venice Boardwalk, California**

*9*

# An Entrée in a Casing

When Jody Maroni began hawking his sausage sandwiches on the Venice Beach boardwalk in the early 1980s, no one had ever heard of a chicken and duck sausage made with fresh cilantro, beer, and serrano chiles. No one, especially not committed sausage-eaters, cared if their favorite food came with or without nitrates and preservatives, was low in fat, or was handmade in the style of a local butcher.

Nevertheless, there he was, standing in front of a barbecue acting like some modern-day Elmer Gantry. He exhorted all passersby to try his individual brand of sausage in the best carny style on the boardwalk:

"Hey you! You need a sausage sandwich! Comeonoverhere and try something new, something different, something I know you'll like. Try a free sample of the best sausage in the world!"

At that time, the Venice boardwalk teemed with all manner of people: local bohemians and artists, surfers, bums, and curious tourists from all over the world coming to steal a peek at Southern California's legendary denizens. Few could turn down his offer—his overt charm was more Coney Island than L.A. mellow, but it lured people in by the hundreds. With his wild array of sausages (a foodstuff as old as time and intrinsic to all cultures of the world), Jody was a part of the boardwalk. He helped make it what it was then and is today: an energetic and culturally diverse microcosm—a world circus.

Hot Italian or Polish sausage was one thing, but who had ever heard of a chicken and duck sausage made with lemon and caraway seeds? Or Chinese-style chicken and duck with sesame oil. His flavors reflected not only the many cultures who came by his barbecue, but changing trends in food as well.

It was a time of flux and great creativity in the food world. Always health-conscious, Californians were beginning to experiment with the foods of their melting-pot culture. Jody's Yucatan Chicken & Duck with Cilantro & Beer reflected the growing demand for southwest food, while Louisiana Boudin Hot Links came directly from the Bayou with a California twist (including rice, green onions, and loads of chile pepper). Figs, Marsala Wine, & Pine Nuts was reminiscent of a stuffing for the holiday bird. Because he noted the trend away from red meats and increased awareness of high fat content and chemical additives, Jody made some important changes to the classic sausage. He added more poultry flavors, reduced the fat content far below the previous industry standard, and never used any form of nitrates or preservatives. Jody learned new ways to blend fruits, vegetables, and fresh meat and put them into a sausage casing. He started grinding his sausage coarsely so you could actually see and identify the ingredients, and used reduced stocks to replace the flavor and juiciness that was lost by drastically cutting the fat content. He was soon moving far beyond the emulsified sausage that most people were familiar with.

By the mid 1980s, Jody had gone from being a rebellious street hawker to running a popular fast-food window on the boardwalk. He perfected the sandwich that has since made him famous by adding a New York style jumble of grilled onions and peppers, and serving it in a freshly baked onion-poppyseed roll made by a local Jewish baker. And every day his efforts were noticed farther and farther from the boardwalk.

By 1987 his wholesale business was flourishing and Jody leased a USDA factory where he could create new sausage flavors. The next to appear were Bombay Curried Lamb, Moroccan Lamb with Tangerines, Wine, & Currants, Chicken & Duck with Basil & Sun-dried Tomatoes, and Pork with Prosciutto, Sun-dried Tomatoes, & Pine Nuts. Simultaneously, the multitudes who had visited his now numerous stands were mail-ordering Maroni's by the pound and having them shipped all over the country. It wasn't long before stores like Trader Joe's and Ralph's in the West, and Zabar's in the East were featuring his sausages.

Today, Maroni sells his sausages to grocers, restaurants, hotels, and caterers all across the country. There is a Jody Maroni on Universal CityWalk, one of Southern California's prime tourist destinations; and he's now at Los Angeles International Airport, too. His sausage sandwich is sold at The Great Western Forum (home to Kings and Lakers games), UCLA, The Greek Theater, Warner Brothers Studios, and The San Diego Zoo. Hospitals all over Southern California feature Maroni's sausages, which says something about the healthy nature of the product.

Sausages have made a comeback—they are undergoing a wild renaissance in popularity and are now available almost everywhere. Most supermarkets now feature an extensive display of sausages of every description, it's not just hot or sweet Italian anymore.

## Important Information on Cooking with Today's Lower-fat Sausages

In the past, virtually all sausage recipes directed you to prick the sausages before cooking, whether you were about to poach, bake, grill, broil, or fry them. This was to release some of the fat prior to cooking and does *not* apply to today's lower-fat sausages.

Traditional pork sausage was made with about a fifty percent fat ratio to the meat. Today's sausages range from around eleven percent for the poultry sausage and top out somewhere around thirty percent for the all-pork sausages. But fat was added to sausages for a reason: flavor. In order to replace that flavor without the fat, Jody Maroni and the other sausagemakers fueling the revolution in healthier sausage have added things like reduced stocks, dried fruit, and fresh herbs.

These sausages do not need to be pricked to release the excess fat because there is no excess fat, only the precious meat juices, stocks, and flavorings that keep your sausage from tasting like cooked sawdust, which is how some completely fat-free sausages have been described.

As a result, when cooking with the "new" sausages we will continue to remind you: please do not overcook your sausages! When we direct you to precook the sausages (page 14), they will be cooked through and safe to eat after that process is finished—the grilling, griddling, or broiling that follows is simply to crisp the skin and give the sausage a golden, slightly charred, and crunchy exterior.

When following recipes from other books and magazines which call for sausages (either in or out of their casings), always reduce the cooking time substantially if you are using a reduced-fat sausage.

Never poke holes in a sausage— It's bad!

—Jody Maroni

the sausage

stands
ALONE

# A Step-by-Step Guide to Grilling Sausages

## OUTDOOR GRILLING:

**1** In general, before you grill your sausages, it is advisable to precook them (see note below). Precooked sausages will take anywhere from 3 to 5 minutes to grill, depending on your equipment and the heat level.

**2** If you are lucky enough to have a backyard barbecue grill, prepare a fire as usual or preheat a gas grill to medium heat. If necessary, scrape the grill to dislodge any built-up food particles using a tool designed for the purpose, which is available from most barbecue equipment manufacturers. If your grill rack is fairly new, wipe it with a rag dampened with cooking oil to prevent the sausages from sticking. To prevent flare-ups that result from dripping fats and juices, you have two choices: **A.)** bank the coals around the edges of the barbecue and place a drip pan in the center, or **B.)** keep a spray bottle of water on hand to douse any flare-ups as they occur (substituting beer, fruit juice, and/or wine for the water in your spray bottle will add a burst of flavor every time you spray the coals).

**3** When the fire is ready, place the sausages on the hot grilling surface. Use sturdy, long-handled tongs (12 inches is a good size) to turn your sausages as they sizzle and char. Using a fork would pierce the skin and allow too many of the precious juices to run off (which would also cause increased flare-ups). Turn the sausages about every 2 to 3 minutes, ensuring that the char lines from the grill are evenly distributed on all sides. When using reduced-fat sausages, it is important not to overcook them, or they will become dry and lose some of their flavor. A good doneness test is the same one used for steaks: after a few minutes of cooking, turning occasionally, press the sausage gently with your finger; when it feels as firm as the tip of your nose, it's done (if you aren't sure, or it takes you awhile to get the hang of the "press" test, remember that the internal temperature of the cooked sausage should read 160°F on an instant-read thermometer). Let the sausages rest for a minute or two on a platter before serving with your favorite side dishes and condiments.

## INDOOR GRILLING:

Outdoor grilling is definitely our preferred method for cooking sausage, but not everyone has an outdoor grill. Of course most people do have a broiler, but before we'd recommend broiling sausage, there is a better alternative that gives results almost as good as an outdoor grill. The heavy cast-iron ridged griddle pan has recently been gaining in popularity as a low-fat method of cooking meat, poultry, and fish. These pans come from several manufacturers in several sizes; our favorite is the reversible double griddle pan. It straddles two burners, making for plenty of cooking surface. One side of the pan is smooth (perfect for pancakes), and the other side has diagonal ridges. Both sides have a channel around the outside so that the fat runs off, leaving the sausages to grill alone, not resting in fat as they would in a frying pan. If the griddle pan is well seasoned (follow the manufacturers instructions included with the pan), there is no need to add any fat before grilling. For the first 5 to 10 times you use your griddle pan, however, it is advisable to spray lightly with cooking spray, until the natural nonstick surface has developed. Never use harsh detergents on your cast-iron cookware—soak briefly in very hot water, then scrub with a medium-bristle dishbrush, using a tiny amount of very mild detergent only if necessary. Be sure to dry the pan thoroughly before putting it away. We put ours in the oven where the gas pilot light provides enough heat to dry it completely. Best of all, a ridged griddle will make attractive and crunchy char lines on your whole sausage or sausage slices. See page 16 for instructions on broiling.

## Precooking:

Precooking a fresh sausage serves two purposes: it renders out some of the fat so that the sausage doesn't spit and cause flare-ups on the grill, and it provides for a more even cooking of the sausage. For an attractive, slightly charred exterior, it's best to cook sausage at high heat, but without some form of precooking, the outside would be crisp and golden while the inside is still undercooked.

There are two methods of precooking sausages: baking and poaching. Depending on how much time you have, you can either bake the sausages in a preheated 350°F oven for 15 to 20 minutes, or poach them (simmer gently) for 5 minutes. We like to use a mixture of either wine, fruit juice, or beer for the poaching liquid, depending on the sausage being used and the recipe (it's another way to add a little flavor). At this point you may either let the sausages drain on paper towels for up to 30 minutes before grilling, griddling, or broiling them, or proceed directly to the chosen cooking process.

I cannot in good conscience recommend precooking sausages in the microwave.

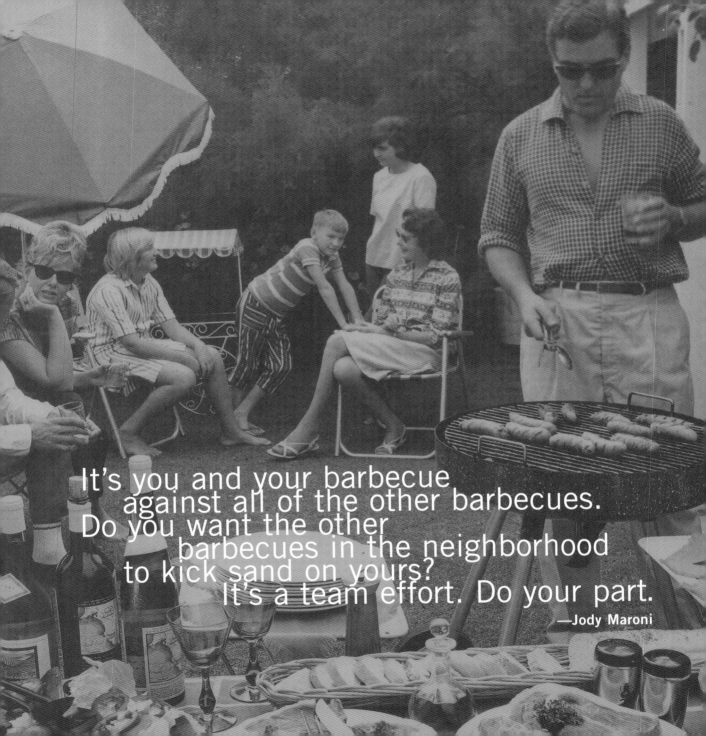

It's you and your barbecue against all of the other barbecues. Do you want the other barbecues in the neighborhood to kick sand on yours? It's a team effort. Do your part.

—Jody Maroni

# Other Ways to Cook a World Famous Sausage all by Itself

## THE EVERYDAY METHODS

### Frying:

For many years one of the most common ways to cook sausage, frying still has its benefits. There is no need to build a fire or heat a grill, and it may be the ideal way to cook breakfast sausages to accompany scrambled eggs, toast, and freshly squeezed orange juice.

In a large nonstick or well-seasoned cast-iron skillet, place the sausages so they are not touching each other. Heat the pan over medium-low heat and cook the sausages, turning them often with tongs (don't use a fork or you will lose too many of the tasty juices). Depending on the size of the sausages, they will take from 10 to 15 minutes to cook through. Today's reduced-fat sausages can be dry if overcooked, so take care to remove from the heat as soon as they are done (if you aren't sure, the interior should register 160°F on an instant-read thermometer). Drain briefly on a paper towel-lined plate and serve.

In the 1959 movie *The Black Orchid*, Anthony Quinn's bitter and unfriendly daughter, played by Ina Balin, finally warms to his new love Sophia Loren after the older Loren advises her to "just add a little water to the pan when frying sausages, dear." We often do so when frying our sausages and couldn't agree more. By the time the sausages are done the water has evaporated and the skin becomes beautifully crisp and golden.

### Broiling:

After precooking (see page 14), preheat the broiler to very high heat. On a rack or sheet of aluminum foil with the shiny side up, broil the sausages for about 4 minutes, turning as necessary with tongs. Don't use a fork or you risk piercing the skin and allowing the precious juices to run off. The sausages have been cooked in the prebaking process—broiling serves only to crisp the skin, so be careful not to overcook, or they may become dry.

### Baking:

For the best results, it is important to precook sausages before grilling them, as noted on page 14. But, you can also cook sausages all the way through in the oven. Preheat the oven to 350°F and place the sausages in a roasting pan so that they are not touching each other. Bake for 10 minutes. Increase the heat to 425°F and cook for 10 to 15 minutes more, until done through. Important note: today's reduced-fat sausages can be dry if overcooked, so take care to remove from the oven as soon as they are done (if you aren't sure, the interior should register 160°F on an instant-read thermometer).

## THE ESOTERIC METHODS

Sausage has been around since soon after man first roasted his day's catch over a fire outside the family cave. When the prime cuts of meat had been consumed, the rest of the carcass was chopped, stuffed inside a length of handy intestine, and smoked over the embers of the fire so it would keep longer. Sure, you can spear a sausage with a long, sharp stick and hold it on the edge of your modern-day campfire until it's crisp, charred, and juicy, but here are a couple of other interesting ways to cook a fresh wurst.

### Sausage Under the Ashes

The next time you are having a big, roaring fire in your fireplace, assemble four friends and the following:

**1 pound fresh, reduced-fat sausage**
**(in links or in one long piece, if you have made it yourself)**
**2 ½ cups red wine, preferably Beaujolais**
**1 pound large, well scrubbed potatoes**

Wrap the sausage loosely in a large, doubled sheet of heavy-duty aluminum foil. Roll one end tightly to seal, making a funnel shape with the other end. Pour in the wine and seal the open end tightly (if desired, add some bay leaves, cloves, or orange segments before sealing). Dampen 5 sheets of newspaper and enclose the package inside. Scrape the hot coals to the side underneath the grate and tuck the package in between. Surround the package with the potatoes; both should be resting directly on the hot fireplace floor. Cover the package and the potatoes with some of the hot ashes and coals and leave to cook for 30 minutes.

Brush away the ashes and remove the package and the potatoes. Brush the potatoes well and serve with the sausage, which will have a lovely caramelized wine flavor.

## Camping Out
## with Sausages

Rather than spearing your sausage on a stick, which will release the precious juices that keep today's low-fat sausages moist and delicious, there are several options for camp-cooking sausages.

Try out the Sausage Under the Ashes recipe (if you are the kind that brings wine on a camping trip—if not, substitute beer or apple juice). Or, wrap the sausages tightly in foil without any liquid and precook in the coals for 15 minutes before unwrapping and crisping briefly in a very hot cast-iron skillet.

If you prefer, you can fry the sausages from the raw stage directly in the skillet, but this must be done at a low heat for about 25 minutes. Luckily, one thing we always have a lot of on a camping trip is time. We suggest using a little water in the skillet at first (see page 16), just like Sophia Loren, although it's hard to imagine Sophia camping.

If you are an ambitious camp cook, precook sausages and potatoes at home, cut into 2-inch chunks and thread them onto wooden or metal skewers with peppers and onions. Then, wrap the skewers in foil and drizzle with a little of your favorite bottled vinaigrette before sealing securely for transport. Once at the campsite, unwrap the skewers and crisp quickly on a grate over your campfire. Cleanup at the site is zero! (See the recipe on page 16 for a guide to times and quantities, but don't try to use bread cubes on a camp-out skewer—they will become soggy during transport.)

The first sausage of the summer sets the tone for the entire season. Choose carefully!
—Jody Maroni

# Pairing Beer with Sausage
## by Michael Jackson

What to drink with sausages? Wine is fine but tradition favors beer. Not just any old beer, though. These days, with microbrews in so many styles, it is possible to pick the beer to match the sausage. With a delicate Boudin Blanc, for example, serve a light lemony-tasting wheat beer. Because they are very pale, and sometimes intentionally hazy, these are sometimes known as "white" beers. A good example, quite widely available, is the coriander-tinged Celis White, from Austin, Texas. Or look out, even on American brewers' labels, for the French, Dutch, or German words Blanche, Wit, or Weisse, all meaning "white," or Weizen ("wheat").

With a juicy Bratwurst, go for a golden, Munich-style lager with some malty sweetness and texture. Good examples are Capital Lager, from Madison, Wisconsin (the ancestral home state of the American brat) and Hubsch Lager, from Davis, California. This style of lager is sometimes identified by the German word Helles (meaning, simply, "pale," or "gold").

Some sausages contain maple; so do some beers. The Maple Stout of the Golden Prairie brewery, in Chicago, is a good example. With a lightly spiced pork sausage, go for the herbal hoppiness of a Pale Ale. A good example is Geary's Pale Ale, from Portland, Maine (ignore the lobster on the label). In Seattle, the Pike brewery has occasionally made a Pale Ale with an oregano spicing; it is called Birra Perfetto.

Sausages with stronger herbal, spicy, or fruity flavors need a bigger, richer beer. Dark malts can impart nutty, or anise-like flavors. This works best in a smooth, clean Dark Lager. Sprecher's Bavarian Black, from Milwaukee, Wisconsin, is a good example. If the sausages are really hot, try Dixie's Blackened Voodoo, from New Orleans. Or even a chili beer, like Pike's occasional Cerveza Rosanna, or the Mexicali of the Rogue brewery, in Newport, Oregon.

Some sausages have smoky flavors; as do some beers. This is achieved when the barley grains are dried over a peat or wood fire in the malting procedure. Good examples are Rogue Smoke, or Alaskan Smoked Porter, from Juneau.

It is tempting to recommend an India Pale Ale with Bombay curried sausage, but the typically grapefruity hop varieties often used in this style might be just too tart. Perhaps the answer is to serve something like the Brooklyn Brewery's East Indian Pale Ale as an aperitif to your beer-and-sausage tasting. For dessert, a sausage-shaped cannoli and Brooklyn's Chocolate stout.

# The Jody Maroni
## Sausage Sandwich

MAKES 6 SANDWICHES

This famous sandwich has served thousands of hungry passersby on the Venice boardwalk since the early 80s, and in more recent years can be found in many, many other locations (see page 10). A sandwich with such a following must be delicious, and after talking with The Sausage King himself, it's easy to see why. A deceptively simple recipe, Jody takes care at every step that it's made *his* way, the right way, so that the buns are the perfect chewy consistency inside with just the right amount of crunch on the outside. The pepper and onion mixture is lovingly tended and painstakingly seasoned, and the sausage is cooked to the perfect temperature before being briefly and expertly charred on an extra-hot grill.

Without too much trouble, you can reproduce this famous sandwich at home and, though it might not be *exactly* the same, dreaming of the crowded, crazy scene on the Venice boardwalk while you eat it will certainly help. . . . For the best results, Jody recommends using an outdoor grill. Remember that after prebaking, the sausage is done through and safe to eat. The grilling process is *simply* to *crisp the skin*, so don't be tempted to leave your sausages on the grill for too long. The great flavor of today's sausages is in the spices, reduced stocks, and fruits instead of fat, but because of the reduced fat they will dry out faster (if overcooked) than traditional, higher-fat content sausages. Remember, these aren't your mother's sausages! You could substitute a sourdough, French, or Italian roll for the onion/poppy seed roll, but make sure it is not too much longer than the sausage itself, and don't use a roll with a very hard crust.

1 1/2 tablespoons peanut oil
1 1/4 pounds onions, sliced about 1/4-inch thick
2 green bell peppers, cored, seeded, and cut into 1/4-inch strips
1 red bell pepper, cored, seeded, and cut into 1/4-inch strips
1/2 yellow pepper, cored, seeded, and cut into wide strips
(if unavailable, use 2 red peppers)
Salt and freshly ground black pepper, to taste
1/2 teaspoon garlic powder
1/4 teaspoon dried oregano, crumbled
6 links Jody Maroni or other fresh, reduced-fat sausage (assorted flavors)
6 (six-inch) onion/poppy seed torpedo rolls

In a large cast-iron or nonstick skillet, heat the oil over medium-low heat and add the onions. Sauté very slowly, stirring occasionally, until translucent, about 5 minutes. Add the peppers, salt, pepper, garlic powder, and oregano. Continue to cook gently for 5 to 10 minutes more, until all the vegetables are tender and sweet. Remove from the heat and proceed immediately to prebaking the sausage, or cool the mixture to room temperature and refrigerate, covered, for up to 24 hours (if you refrigerate the mixture, you will have to reheat it gently in the pan before topping your sandwiches).

Prebake the sausages at 350°F for 15 minutes, to an internal temperature of just under 160°F (see the instructions on precooking sausage on page 14). It is best to grill the sausages immediately after prebaking them, but if you must, you can hold them in a warm oven for up to 1 hour.

Preheat a grill, griddle pan, or broiler to high heat. Reheat the onion/pepper mixture if it has cooled. Slice the torpedo rolls open lengthwise, leaving them attached along one long edge. Place the rolls on the grill cut side down and grill just until golden, watching carefully. Place the sausages on the grill, and grill for 2 to 3 minutes *only*, turning with tongs to mark the sausages evenly and taking care not to pierce the skin and release the precious juices. Mound some of the hot onion/pepper mixture evenly along the length of the rolls and top each one with a sausage. Close the rolls, serve, and wait for the applause.

*19*

h

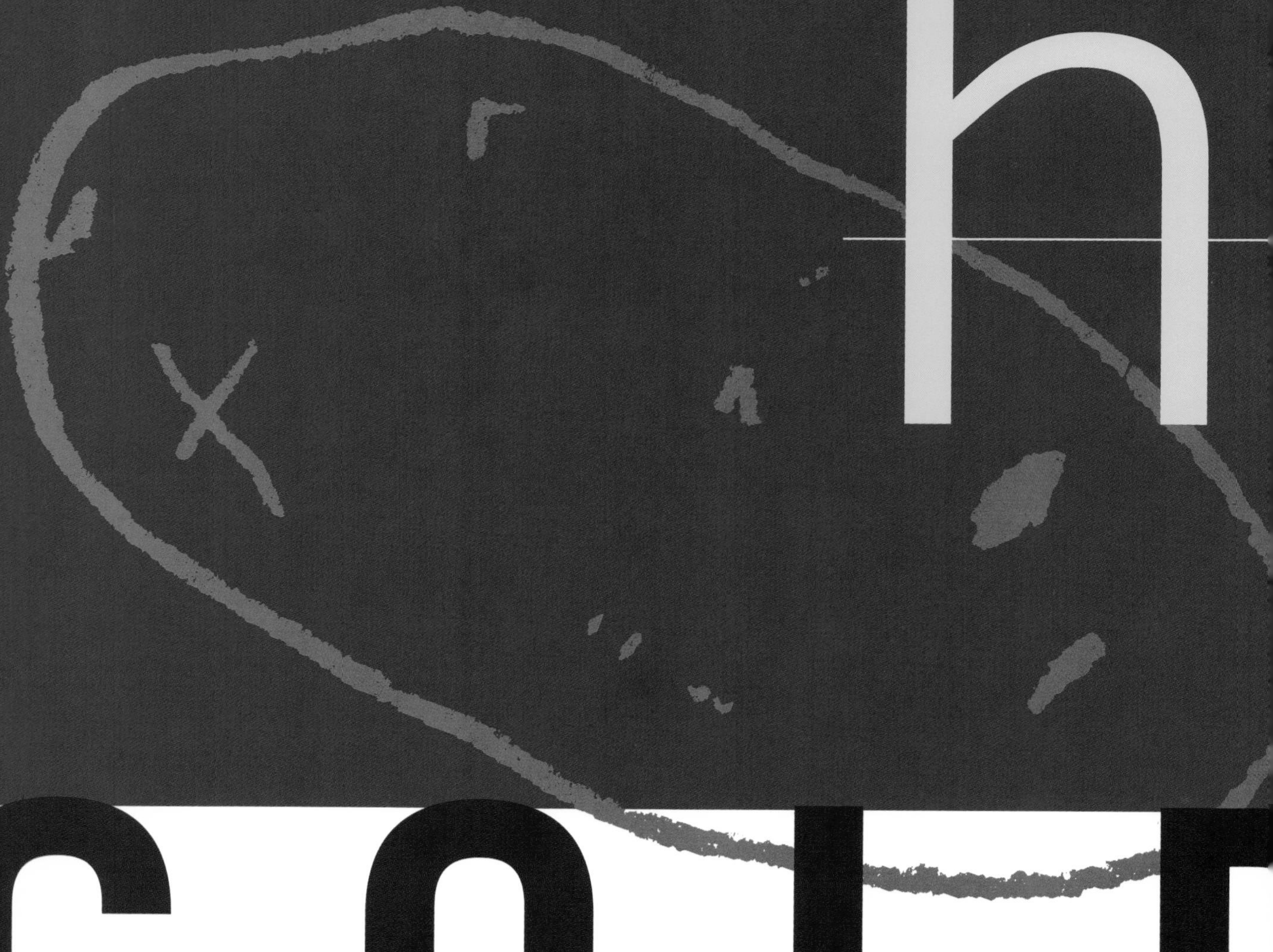

COLD

ot

potatoes

*potatoes*

# Roasted Potatoes with Chipotle and Cilantro

SERVES 6

Roasted potatoes are an easy and versatile dish that many good cooks throw together without even using a recipe. They make a great side dish for grilled or roasted sausages—in fact, you could even place a few sausages on a rack above the potatoes, and cook them at the same time.

The trick of scoring the cut end of the potato with a fork is from England: it creates more surface area to get crusty and crunchy. Canned *chipotles en adobo* are now widely available in regular and specialty markets. Use any small, waxy potato for this dish.

1 1/2 teaspoons coarse sea salt
2 pounds red or White Rose potatoes, well scrubbed
2 to 3 canned chipotle chiles in adobo sauce
2 tablespoons extra-virgin olive oil
1/4 teaspoon freshly ground black pepper, or to taste
Juice of 1 lime
1 teaspoon finely chopped fresh parsley

Bring a saucepan of water to a boil and add 1/2 teaspoon of the salt. If the potatoes are larger than golf balls, cut them in half. Boil the potatoes for 7 minutes, then drain in a colander.

Preheat the oven to 400°F. When the potatoes are cool enough to handle, cut them in half, if you have not already done so, and score the cut ends with a fork to make ridges.

In a mini food processor or a blender, combine the chipotles with a few tablespoons of their sauce and the oil. Purée until smooth, then scrape into a medium-sized bowl. Add the potatoes, the remaining salt, and pepper and toss to evenly coat the potatoes. With a slotted spoon, transfer the potatoes to a roasting pan just large enough to hold them in one layer. Roast for 30 to 45 minutes, tossing the potatoes every 10 minutes, until they are soft and creamy inside and crusty brown on the outside. Squeeze the lime juice over the potatoes, sprinkle with parsley, and serve immediately.

**Variations:**

1. Sprinkle 1/4 cup grated cotija or Jack cheese over the potatoes and return them to the *turned-off* oven for 5 minutes, with the door ajar.

2. Boil whole unpeeled garlic cloves with the potatoes and roast together as above. If they start to brown before the potatoes are done, remove them, then return them to the pan when the potatoes are done.

# Horseradish
# Dill Potato Salad

Today's reduced-fat, gourmet sausages are perfect candidates for your health-conscious backyard grilling in the summertime. You could serve them as part of a mixed grill along with burgers, steaks, and chicken, or do a sausage smorgasbord! (I once had a barbecue featuring seven different varieties of Jody Maroni's.) To round out the menu, combine this creamy, tangy salad with the Grilled Corn Relish (page 43), Pickled Shallots (page 41), and a simple green salad to make a splendid menu for one of summer's long, hot, dog-day afternoons. Added bonus for too-hot cooks: this salad, the relish, and the onions all benefit from being made ahead of time!

**Coarse sea salt**
**3 pounds small red or White Rose potatoes, scrubbed**
**$1/2$ cup water**
**$1/4$ cup sour cream**
**2 tablespoons mayonnaise**
**1 tablespoon Dijon-style mustard**
**2 teaspoons white wine vinegar**
**1 tablespoon bottled horseradish, drained, or 2 tablespoons grated**
**fresh horseradish (grate just before adding to the dressing)**
**$1/2$ small red onion, very finely chopped**
**$1/3$ cup chopped fresh dill**
**Freshly ground pepper, preferably white, to taste**

Bring a generous amount of water to a boil in a large saucepan and add 1 tablespoon salt. Add the potatoes, reduce the heat, and simmer for about 20 minutes, until tender but not falling apart.

While the potatoes cook, in a large serving bowl, whisk together the water, sour cream, mayonnaise, mustard, vinegar, horseradish, onion, and all but 2 teaspoons of the dill. Stir in about $1/2$ teaspoon of salt, and pepper.

When the potatoes are done, drain them in a colander and, as soon as they are cool enough to handle, slice about $1/2$-inch thick right into the serving bowl over the dressing. Toss the salad gently, taking care not to break up the potatoes too much. Cool to room temperature and refrigerate for at least 1 and up to 2 hours. Let stand for 15 to 20 minutes at room temperature before serving. Taste for seasoning, sprinkle the remaining dill over the top of the salad and serve.

# French Potato Salad

Sausage and potatoes make perfect partners. This is the lightest, cleanest, tastiest potato salad I know, and it's also one of the easiest to prepare. Tossing the potatoes with the dressing while they are still warm releases all the heady aromas of the vinegar, herbs, and olive oil (use a good extra-virgin oil—this is one dish where you'll really notice the difference). To make the potato salad even lighter, substitute chicken broth for half of the oil in the vinaigrette.

**2 pounds small red potatoes, preferably new, or early-season potatoes**
**Coarse sea salt**
**2 tablespoons Champagne vinegar**
**1 tablespoon dry white wine**
**1 teaspoon Dijon-style mustard (optional)**
**Freshly ground black pepper, to taste**
**$1/3$ cup extra-virgin olive oil**
**2 tablespoons coarsely chopped baby arugula leaves**
**or 2 teaspoons chopped fresh thyme**
**1 large shallot, minced**
**2 teaspoons chopped fresh parsley**

Scrub the potatoes and, if they are larger than a golf ball, cut them in half. Bring a large saucepan of water to a boil and add 1 tablespoon salt. Add the potatoes and simmer for about 15 minutes, until they are tender but not mushy.

Meanwhile, in a large serving bowl, whisk together the vinegar, wine, mustard, if using, $1/2$ teaspoon salt, and pepper. Drizzle in the oil in a thin stream, constantly whisking until the dressing has emulsified. Stir in the arugula.

Drain the cooked potatoes and, as soon as they are cool enough to handle, cut them into quarters and place them in the bowl with the dressing. Toss gently to coat the potatoes; add the shallot and parsley, toss again briefly, and set aside at room temperature for 20 minutes to allow the flavors to marry. Toss again gently just before serving to redistribute the dressing.

# The Definitive
## Gratin Dauphinoise
scalloped potatoes to you and me

SERVES 6

In France there is much controversy on the subject of this simple, extremely satisfying dish. To add cheese . . . or not to add cheese? that is the question. In America the sister dish (scalloped potatoes) also may or may not have cheese, but we don't seem to get as worked up about it as the French do. Old recipes from England sprinkle flour on each layer of potatoes, and in the deep, deep South they make their version with "oleo and Pet milk." I think you'll find this version to be very tasty, though you'll want to save it for a day when you've been keeping strictly to your diet for a week or two. . . .

2 pounds large red or White Rose potatoes, peeled
Butter, for the baking dish
1$^1/_2$ cups whipping cream
1$^1/_2$ cups milk
1 tablespoon Dijon-style mustard
$^1/_4$ teaspoon ground nutmeg
1 teaspoon sea salt
Freshly ground white pepper, to taste

Using a very sharp knife or, preferably, a mandoline, slice the potatoes $^1/_4$-inch thick and place in a large bowl of cold water.

Generously butter a large ceramic baking dish and set aside. Preheat the oven to 350°F.

In a saucepan, combine the cream, milk, mustard, nutmeg, salt, and pepper. Over medium heat, bring the mixture to just below the simmering point and remove from the heat.

Drain the sliced potatoes thoroughly in a colander and wipe dry the bowl they were soaking in. Return the potatoes to the bowl and pour the warm cream mixture over them. Toss to coat all the slices evenly. Transfer the mixture to the prepared baking dish and press the potatoes down into an even layer with the back of a large spoon. Bake for 1$^1/_2$ to 2 hours, until the surface is deep golden brown and bubbling (if the potatoes are tender but the top is not browned enough, place under a hot broiler for a minute or two).

july 4

the high holy day

of sum-
mer

'n sausage

# July Fourth.

Just the date conjures up images of picnicking families gathering in the bright daylight to play frisbee, throw a tennis ball for the dog, and cluster around the barbecue-meister resplendent in his or her apron and hat, holding court behind the smoking grill. Plates are balanced on knees, seconds are plentiful, and everyone talks at once. As the dusk begins to fall families come closer together; they sit at the table talking of Fourths of July past, and how Aunt Sue's legendary potato salad gets better every year. Desserts are brought out and ice cream is scooped. Then, for the fireworks everyone gets a second wind as they stand, mouths agape and heads craned back, to watch the sparkling spectacle of another year's celebration of our country's independence. The evening winds down in a slow, contented way, as hampers are packed, kids are sent on rubbish patrol, and cars head slowly home, each one full of sleepy people and one very awake driver.

The menu for a Fourth of July meal can be as American as apple pie or a happy reflection of the wonderful melting pot that's made this country unique. Pick and choose from among the following, and don't forget the legendary dishes that are a part of your own family's ethnic heritage:

Hot and Sweet Italian Sausages ✶ Hamburgers and Hot Dogs ✶ Potato Salad ✶ Pasta Salad
Coleslaw ✶ Corn on the Cob ✶ Big Tomatoes and Red Onions, Sliced Thick (grill the onions if you like)
Pickles, Sweet and Sour ✶ Marinated Vegetables (great filling for the vegetarians' rolls)
Pickle Relish, and all the Mustards, Chutneys, and Salsa you can make, borrow, or buy
Baked Beans ✶ Soft Rolls ✶ Torpedo Rolls ✶ Corn Bread ✶ Fruit Salad in a Hollowed-Out
Watermelon ✶ Cantaloupe and Strawberries ✶ Peaches and Pears in an Ice Bowl ✶ Ice Cream
Chocolate Chip Cookies ✶ Apple Pie ✶ Grasshopper Pie ✶ Lemon Meringue Pie

*27*

bean

grains

# Warm Lentils with Mustard Dressing

SERVES 6

This lentil salad packs a real wallop of flavor. And you thought lentils were a nice, tame health food! This is even better when made ahead of time, so that the flavors can marry, just be gentle about reheating so the dressing doesn't scorch and make the dish dry. It should be nice and juicy.

### Dressing:

1 large garlic clove, sliced
1 medium shallot, sliced
$1/4$ cup sherry vinegar
1 tablespoon capers, rinsed
1 tablespoon dill-flavored or other Dijon-style mustard
$3/4$ teaspoon sea salt
$1/4$ teaspoon freshly ground black pepper
$3/4$ cup extra-virgin olive oil

### Lentils:

1 tablespoon olive oil
2 medium shallots, finely chopped
1 rib celery, finely chopped
1 large carrot, finely chopped
2 garlic cloves, finely chopped
$1 1/2$ cups small French green lentils (Puy lentils)
2 cups low-fat, low-sodium chicken broth
Water as needed
Sea salt and freshly ground black pepper, to taste

*Continued over*

In a blender, combine the garlic, shallot, vinegar, capers, mustard, salt, and pepper. Blend until smooth, scraping down the sides. Add the oil, $1/4$ cup at a time, blending well between each addition and scraping the sides of the container. Set the dressing aside (it will keep in the refrigerator for up to 1 week).

For the lentils, heat a large, heavy saucepan over medium-low heat and add the oil. Sauté the shallots for about 4 minutes, until softened. Add the celery and about three-fourths of the chopped carrot. Stir the vegetables for 3 to 4 minutes, until wilted, then add the garlic. Stir for 1 minute more, until it has released its aroma, then add the lentils. Stir until they are coated with the oil and warmed through, then add the broth. Add enough water so that the lentils are covered by $1/4$ inch of liquid, then raise the heat and bring the mixture to a boil. Reduce the heat, cover the pan and simmer very gently for 15 minutes. Stir in the remaining chopped carrot and cook for 10 minutes more, until the lentils are tender but still with a nice bite to them. Add salt and pepper. Remove from the heat and allow to stand, covered, for 5 minutes. If there is a lot of excess liquid, drain the lentils in a colander, shaking to get rid of all the liquid. While the lentils are still nice and hot, combine them with about half of the dressing and serve immediately, reserving the remaining dressing for another use. Or, if desired, cool to room temperature, cover and refrigerate for up to 4 days. Reheat in a microwave or double boiler before serving.

# Black Beans with Lime and Chipotle

SERVES 6

Chipotle chiles have a smoky, unique flavor that is worth seeking out. They are widely available canned *en adobo*, so that is what I have used here. If you are lucky enough to find the dried variety, soften one in a bowl of very hot water for $1/2$ hour, then trim the ends, remove the seeds, and cut into $1/2$-inch chunks. Then use as directed here (don't forget to use the soaking liquid as part of the bean-cooking liquid).

And don't be alarmed at the quantity of garlic, the cloves will have turned into melt-in-your-mouth nuggets of sweetness by the end of the cooking time. Stir the beans once or twice and they'll disappear into the juicy "sauce". I like to serve this side dish with a decidedly south-of-the-border sausage, like Yucatan Chicken & Duck with Cilantro & Beer, or Chicken & Turkey Chorizo.

2 cups dried black beans, picked over
1 canned chipotle chile *en adobo*, coarsely chopped
2 bay leaves
1 large onion, coarsely chopped
8 large, peeled garlic cloves, whole
$1^1/2$ teaspoons dried thyme, crumbled
$1/2$ teaspoon sea salt
Freshly ground black pepper, to taste
2 limes, 1 halved and 1 cut into thin wedges
3 green onions, white and light green parts only, thinly sliced
3 to 4 radishes, trimmed and thinly sliced (optional)

In a large saucepan, cover the beans with 7 cups of water. Cover the pan and bring to a boil over high heat. Boil for 2 minutes, then remove from the heat and leave to soak, still covered, for 2 hours. Drain the beans, return them to the pan and cover with 6 cups fresh cold water. Add the chile, bay leaves, onion, garlic, and thyme. Over high heat, bring to a boil, then reduce the heat so the liquid is just simmering. Simmer gently, skimming off the foam occasionally, for 30 minutes. Add the salt and pepper and cook for 30 minutes to $2^1/2$ hours more (the cooking time will depend on the age of the beans—they should be tender but not mushy or falling apart). Watch the pan and add water as necessary if it falls below the level of the beans. Remove from the heat and let cool in the liquid. Discard the bay leaves.

At this point, the beans will improve in flavor if refrigerated for up to 2 days. Reheat gently, thoroughly squeeze the juice from the lime halves into the mixture and serve with a slotted spoon. Garnish each serving with sliced green onion, lime wedges, and sliced radishes.

# Soft Polenta with Mushrooms and Parmesan

SERVES 6

In Italy, polenta has been a traditional accompaniment to sausages for many generations. At the *Carnivale* every year in Tossignano local chefs cook up a vast cauldron containing 440 pounds of polenta and, later, hundreds of pounds of sausage and tomatoes. This golden yellow grain makes the perfect partner for a grilled or baked sausage on a cold winter evening.

1 tablespoon butter
$3/4$ pound white mushrooms, sliced $1/4$ inch thick
1 tablespoon finely chopped fresh parsley
$1 1/2$ tablespoons olive oil
$1/2$ medium-size onion, finely chopped
2 garlic cloves, minced
$4 1/2$ cups low-fat, low-sodium chicken broth
$1 1/2$ cups water
$1 1/2$ teaspoons coarse sea salt
$1 1/2$ cups polenta or coarsely ground yellow corn meal
2 teaspoons finely chopped fresh thyme leaves, or scant 1 teaspoon dried thyme, crumbled
Freshly ground black pepper, to taste
$3/4$ cup freshly grated imported Parmesan cheese

In a small skillet, heat the butter over medium heat. Add the mushrooms and sauté for about 5 minutes, stirring, until softened. Remove from the heat and stir in the parsley. Cover and set aside in a warm place until the polenta is cooked.

In a large, heavy saucepan, heat the oil over medium heat. Sauté the onion and garlic for 5 to 6 minutes, stirring, until softened.

Add the broth, water, and salt to the pan and raise the heat to medium-high. When the liquid is simmering, gradually add the polenta, sprinkling it in a very slow, thin stream, whisking constantly in the same direction until all the grains are incorporated and no lumps remain. Reduce the heat to very low. Switch to a wooden spoon and stir thoroughly every 1 or 2 minutes for 20 to 25 minutes, or until the mixture pulls away from the sides of the pan and the grains of polenta have softened (add 1 or 2 tablespoons of boiling water if the mixture gets too thick to stir before the grains have softened). Stir in the thyme, pepper, and Parmesan and remove from the heat.

Spoon some polenta into each of 6 warmed shallow bowls and top with a spoonful of the sautéed mushrooms. Serve at once.

# Couscous with Red and Yellow Tomatoes

SERVES 4

This is a very refreshing dish, a vaguely Middle-Eastern 'side' that would make the perfect partner for grilled lamb or pork sausages. Serving this salad alongside today's healthy sausages makes a light and healthy menu, and the golden grains and colorful tomatoes are a visually stunning presentation.

1 cup low-fat, low-sodium chicken broth
$^1/_4$ cup water
2 tablespoons orange juice
2 tablespoons olive oil
2 tablespoons white wine
1 tablespoon Champagne or white wine vinegar
1 cup instant couscous
$^1/_2$ small red onion, thinly sliced, and slices quartered
2 tablespoons capers, rinsed and drained
1 tablespoon finely chopped fresh mint
$^1/_2$ teaspoon sea salt
Freshly ground black pepper, to taste
2 medium-size, ripe red tomatoes, cored, seeded if desired, and coarsely chopped
2 medium-size, ripe yellow tomatoes, cored, seeded if desired, and coarsely chopped (or substitute 2 more red tomatoes)
Sprigs of fresh mint, for garnish (optional)

Bring the broth, water, orange juice, 1 tablespoon of the olive oil, the wine, and the vinegar to a boil and remove from the heat. Place the couscous in a metal mixing bowl and pour the hot liquid over the top. Cover the bowl and let sit for 20 minutes, then add the remaining oil and fluff with a fork to separate the grains. Stir in the onion, capers, mint, salt, and pepper. Chill the mixture for at least 1 and up to 3 hours.

Remove the salad from the refrigerator 30 minutes before serving. Taste for seasoning. Mound the mixture on a platter and surround with the tomatoes. Garnish with sprigs of mint, if desired, and serve.

*35*

# Persian Rice Pilaf

SERVES 6

Back when 'Persian' meant shady orange groves and Omar Khayyam instead of the Ayatollah, rice dishes always featured fresh and dried fruits and nuts, part of the great Middle Eastern cooking tradition. This light but complex pilaf would make a striking partner for Jody Maroni's Sausage with Figs, Marsala, & Pine Nuts, the Bombay Curried Sausage with Monoucka Raisins or, best of all, the Moroccan Sausage with Tangerines, Wine, & Currants.

3 tablespoons canola or vegetable oil
1 medium-size onion, coarsely chopped
$1/2$ cup blanched, slivered almonds
$1 1/2$ cups long-grain rice
1 tablespoon finely chopped orange zest
$1/3$ cup diced dates
3 cups low-fat, low-sodium chicken broth, warmed
$1/2$ teaspoon sea salt
Freshly ground black pepper
2 tablespoons chopped Italian flat-leaf parsley

In a large heavy saucepan, heat the oil over medium heat. Add the onion and the almonds and cook, stirring occasionally, until the onion is softened and the almonds are just golden. Add the rice and stir all the ingredients together for about 2 minutes, coating the rice evenly but not allowing it to brown. Stir in the orange zest, dates, broth, and salt and bring the mixture to a boil.

Immediately reduce the heat to very low so the mixture is just simmering. Cover the pan and cook for about 20 minutes without stirring, until little holes have appeared in the surface of the rice and all the liquid has evaporated. At this point, if desired, you can hold the pilaf for up to 10 minutes, covered and off the heat. To serve, stir in pepper, to taste, and the parsley. Taste again for seasoning and serve.

# Get your red hauts!

—Jody Maroni

# salsas

relishes

# Salsa Cruda

YIELD: ABOUT 4 CUPS

White onions are better than yellow for making salsa, since their flavor will not intensify and overwhelm the mixture as it sits. Two hours resting time is ideal—after 4 hours this simple salsa will begin to lose its fresh, crunchy quality. The basil in this salsa perfectly accompanies Mediterranean-style sausages; substitute cilantro when using sausages with a south-of-the-border identity. The fresh mint is a real eye-opener—dried mint is not a substitute.

Core the tomatoes, squeeze out their seeds, and cut them into $1/4$-inch dice. In a glass or ceramic bowl combine the tomatoes with the other ingredients. Toss gently and taste for seasoning. Cover and refrigerate for 2 to 3 hours before serving. Just before serving, taste again for seasoning and adjust if necessary. If you like a juicier salsa, add $1/4$ cup additional ice water.

2 pounds ripe, but firm, plum tomatoes
$1/2$ small white onion, cut into $1/4$-inch dice
2 garlic cloves, very finely chopped
1 serrano chile, stemmed, seeded, and minced (optional)
3 tablespoons finely chopped fresh basil or cilantro
2 tablespoons finely chopped fresh mint
1 tablespoon extra-virgin olive oil
$1/4$ cup ice water
$1/2$ teaspoon sea salt, or to taste
$1/4$ teaspoon freshly ground black pepper, or to taste

# Pickled Shallots

YIELD: 3 CUPS

You can substitute any small onions that are available in the market—cipolline, pearl onions, or even small red onions—just make sure none of them have sprouted. These flavor-packed babies really liven up a simple grilled sausage and a wedge of country bread—so I say there is no reason not to have some in the refrigerator at all times!

3 cups firm, medium-sized shallots (about 2 pounds)
$^1/_2$ cup dry red wine
$^1/_2$ cup balsamic vinegar
$^1/_2$ cup red wine vinegar
$^1/_2$ cup sugar
2 tablespoons coarse sea salt
2 tablespoons black peppercorns
1 tablespoon mustard seeds
Pinch of crushed red pepper flakes
1 to 2 cups water, as needed

If using shallots, cipolline, or pearl onions: bring a large saucepan of water to a boil and blanch them for 1 minute. Drain in a colander and when cool enough to handle, slide off the skins and trim the root ends neatly.

If using red onions, peel and quarter them.

In a medium saucepan, combine the wine, vinegars, sugar, salt, peppercorns, mustard seeds, and the pepper flakes. Stir over low heat until the sugar has dissolved. Add the shallots and enough of the water so that the liquid covers them. Bring the liquid to a boil. Reduce the heat to low and simmer partially covered for 15 minutes, then remove from the heat and let cool to room temperature. Transfer the shallots and all the liquid to a sterilized glass jar, cover tightly, and keep refrigerated for up to 2 weeks.

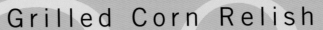

# Grilled Corn Relish

YIELD: 3 CUPS

If fresh shiitake mushrooms are not available, substitute fresh porcini, portabello, or field mushrooms, using enough to yield about $3/4$ cup of chopped mushrooms.

5 sun-dried tomato halves
$1/2$ cup extra-virgin olive oil
1 large garlic clove, finely chopped
$1/2$ teaspoon ground cumin
$1/4$ teaspoon chili powder, preferably guajillo or chipotle
$1/4$ teaspoon sea salt, or to taste
$1/4$ teaspoon freshly ground black pepper, or to taste
3 ears white or yellow corn, shucked
1 teaspoon canola oil
7 medium shiitake mushrooms, tough stems removed, coarsely chopped
2 tablespoons finely chopped cilantro
2 tablespoons fresh lime juice
1 to 2 teaspoons Tabasco sauce, or to taste

Place the sun-dried tomatoes in a measuring cup and cover with very hot water. Prepare a medium-hot fire for grilling and preheat the oven to 450°F (if you do not have a charcoal grill, preheat a well-seasoned ridged cast-iron griddle). In a small bowl, whisk together $1/4$ cup of the oil, the garlic, cumin, chili powder, salt, and pepper. Place each ear of corn on a 15-inch long sheet of aluminum foil and brush with the oil mixture. Wrap firmly

*Continued over*

and roast in the oven for 10 minutes.

Unwrap the corn and grill the ears for 5 to 10 minutes, turning to brown each side evenly. Watch the corn carefully, it should be nicely charred but not blackened.

When the corn is cool enough to handle, place each ear over a large bowl and cut off the kernels, keeping the blade angled so you get the whole kernel but none of the tough cob.

In a small nonstick skillet, heat the canola oil over medium heat. Add the chopped mushrooms and sauté until dry and slightly golden, about 5 minutes. Season to taste and transfer the mushrooms to the bowl with the corn.

Squeeze the tomatoes dry and chop them finely. Add the remaining $1/4$ cup olive oil, chopped tomatoes, cilantro, lime juice, and Tabasco to the corn mixture. Toss together and refrigerate for at least 6 hours and up to 2 days before serving.

Hey you!
Comeonoverhere
and try one!

—Jody Maroni

# appetizers

egg
dishes

# Garlic Sausage and Rosemary Ravioli

Using wonton wrappers to make ravioli changed my life; it is so much easier than making and rolling out pasta, you'll be tempted to make ravioli every night of the week. Any combination of finely chopped, well-drained ingredients can be stuffed inside ravioli. Just remember that cooking time in the water is brief, so all ingredients should be fully cooked before you assemble the ravioli.

If desired, dress the ravioli with some good-quality store-bought tomato sauce.

3 links (about $3/4$ pound total) fresh, reduced-fat garlic-flavored pork sausage, such as Jody Maroni's Toulouse Garlic, casings removed
1 cup ricotta cheese
1 large egg, lightly beaten
2 tablespoons grated imported Parmesan cheese (optional)
2 teaspoons finely chopped fresh rosemary
$1/4$ teaspoon sea salt
$1/8$ teaspoon freshly ground black pepper
1 package round wonton wrappers (gyoza)
2 tablespoons fruity extra-virgin olive oil
1 teaspoon finely chopped fresh parsley

*Continued over*

Heat a large nonstick or cast-iron skillet over medium heat. Add the sausage and cook, crumbling and separating the meat with a wooden spoon, until only just cooked through, about 6 minutes. Do not overcook or the sausage will be dry. With a slotted spoon, transfer the sausage meat to a double layer of paper towels to drain and cool.

In a bowl, combine the ricotta, egg, Parmesan, if using, rosemary, salt, and pepper. Stir the sausage thoroughly into the ricotta mixture.

Making 2 ravioli at a time, place 2 wonton wrappers on a dry work surface. Spoon about 2 teaspoons of filling into a mound in the center of each wrapper and brush the edges lightly with water. Wet the edges of 2 more wrappers and place them, one at a time, over the filling, matching up the edges. Press the mound of filling down gently and then press the edges of the wrappers firmly together, easing out any air that might be inside the ravioli. Press the tines of a fork all the way around the edges to make a firm seal. Repeat with the remaining wrappers and filling, making a total of about 24 ravioli. Wrap the remaining wonton wrappers tightly and freeze for your next ravioli experiment.

Warm 4 serving bowls in a low oven. Bring a large skillet of lightly salted water to a gentle simmer. Cook the ravioli in batches to prevent overcrowding, for 3 to 4 minutes, until they rise to the surface and look slightly translucent.

When they are cooked, remove the ravioli with a slotted spoon and rest the spoon on paper towels briefly to remove excess water. Transfer about 6 of the ravioli to each of the warm bowls, drizzle with a little of the olive oil and scatter a scant $1/4$ teaspoon parsley over the top of each. Serve immediately.

# Dolmades with Yogurt Sauce

YIELD: ABOUT 30

These little packages are an easy, make-ahead hors d'oeuvres for parties. I like to stick a toothpick in each dolmade to make perfect, tidy finger-food.

1 (8-ounce) jar grape leaves, drained
2 to 3 links (about $1/2$ to $3/4$ pound total) fresh, reduced-fat lamb and fruit sausages, such as Jody Maroni's Moroccan Sausage with Tangerines, Wine, & Currants, casings removed
$2^1/2$ cups cooked long-grain rice
3 tablespoons pine nuts, toasted and coarsely chopped
$1/4$ cup finely chopped fresh flat-leaf parsley
3 tablespoons finely chopped fresh mint
$1/2$ teaspoon sea salt
$1/4$ teaspoon freshly ground black pepper
3 tablespoons olive oil
$1/2$ cup low-fat, low-sodium chicken broth

## Sauce:
1 cup plain yogurt
3 tablespoons finely chopped fresh mint
1 garlic clove, finely chopped
$1/2$ teaspoon sea salt, or to taste
Freshly ground pepper, to taste
Lemon wedges, for serving

Place the grape leaves in a bowl, separate them, and cover with cold water. Let stand for 30 minutes.

Meanwhile, heat a large nonstick or cast-iron skillet over medium heat. Add the sausage and cook, crumbling and separating the meat with a wooden spoon, until only just cooked through, about 6 minutes. Do not overcook or the sausage will be dry. If desired, tilt the pan and spoon off any accumulated fat. Remove the pan from the heat and add the rice, pine nuts, parsley, mint, salt, and pepper. Mix together thoroughly (the mixture will be crumbly).

Trim the tough stems from the grape leaves and place one with the veined side up on a work surface, stem end closest to you. Scoop up 1 rounded tablespoon of the filling and press down firmly with the cupped palm of your other hand to compact the filling into an egg shape. Place the filling on the stem end of the leaf, $1/2$ inch above the edge. Fold the stem end up and over the filling, then fold in the two sides over the filling and roll up the packet starting at the bottom. Place seam side down in the base of a 12-inch skillet and continue making packets until you have used all the filling. The dolmades should be touching each other snugly. At this point the dolmades could be covered and refrigerated for up to 1 day.

Drizzle the oil and the broth over the dolmades. Bring the liquid to a low simmer and cover the pan. Simmer gently for about 30 minutes, or until the liquid is almost all absorbed. Uncover the pan and cool to room temperature. Meanwhile, combine the sauce ingredients in a small bowl.

Serve the dolmades with the sauce and lemon wedges, or refrigerate for up to 1 day and serve chilled or at room temperature.

# Phyllo Triangles with Spinach, Lamb Sausage, and Feta

**MAKES 25 HORS D'OEUVRES**

Phyllo pastry comes from the Middle East and has been enthusiastically adopted by American cooks because of its great flavor, presentation, and extra-easy preparation. These crisp packets are bursting with flavor and make a great pass-around starter for a sausage barbecue. Best of all, they can be frozen for up to 1 week in airtight containers before baking. When you are ready to serve, cook them straight from frozen, adding 5 minutes or so to the cooking time.

Note: If you prefer, use a good quality nonstick spray instead of the butter and oil mixture on each layer of phyllo—it provides a thin but even coverage that would be impossible with a pastry brush. The flavor is not quite as good but it is a good way to shave fat from the dish.

2 links (about $1/2$ pound total) fresh, mild or spicy reduced-fat lamb sausages, such as Jody Maroni's Bombay Curried Sausage, casings removed
2 teaspoons olive oil
1 medium-size onion, finely chopped
$1/2$ pound white or cremini mushrooms, stems removed, wiped clean and coarsely chopped
3 ounces (about $3/4$ cup, crumbled) feta cheese
1 (10-ounce) package frozen spinach, thawed and squeezed thoroughly dry
3 tablespoons chopped fresh flat-leaf parsley
1 large egg, lightly beaten
15 sheets phyllo pastry, thawed
2 tablespoons melted butter
2 tablespoons vegetable oil

Place the sausage in a nonstick or cast-iron skillet and heat over medium-low heat. Cook, breaking up and separating the sausage meat with a wooden spoon, until the meat is only just cooked through and no trace of pink remains, about 6 minutes. Do not overcook or it will be dry. Remove the sausage with a slotted spoon and drain on paper towels. If the sausage is in large chunks, break it up with your fingers into pea-sized pieces.

Discard the fat, if any, in the skillet and wipe it with a paper towel. Add the olive oil and place over medium-low heat. Add the onion and sauté for 5 minutes, then add the mushrooms and cook until softened and dry (increase the heat toward the end of the cooking time to evaporate the excess moisture).

In a large bowl, combine the mushroom mixture with the cooked sausage, feta, spinach, parsley, and egg.

Unwrap the thawed phyllo and cut the whole stack lengthwise into 4-inch-wide strips. Cover the strips with a slightly dampened tea towel. As you work, re-cover the pastry to keep it from drying out and becoming brittle.

Preheat the oven to 350°F and combine the melted butter and the vegetable oil in a small bowl.

Place 1 strip of phyllo lengthwise on the work surface and brush it with the butter mixture. Place about 1 scant tablespoon of the filling 1 inch from the bottom edge. Fold the lower right corner of the pastry up and over the filling, forming a triangle, and continue folding back and forth (as though you were folding a flag) until you reach the end of the strip. Transfer to a lightly oiled baking sheet and brush the top of the triangle with a little more of the butter mixture. Make the remaining triangles in the same way, using 2 baking sheets if necessary.

Bake for 20 minutes, or until the triangles are golden brown. Cool slightly before serving as the filling will be very hot.

# Sausage and Fresh Goat Cheese Purses

SERVES 8

Looking like small Christmas favors, these purses make a spectacular first course and are simpler to prepare than they may at first appear. The crêpes can be made the day before, and the purses assembled up to one hour ahead, before simply heating them through in the oven. Serve two parcels per person.

### Crêpes:

2 large eggs
1 cup all-purpose flour
1 cup milk
Scant $1/2$ cup water
$1/2$ teaspoon sea salt
2 tablespoons butter, melted

### Sauce:

$3/4$ cup sour cream
2 tablespoons finely chopped cilantro
$1/2$ teaspoon sea salt
$1/4$ teaspoon ground cumin (optional)
1 to 2 tablespoons water

Vegetable oil for cooking the crêpes
4 links (about 1 pound total) fresh, reduced-fat poultry sausage, such as Jody Maroni's Chicken Apple with Sherry, casings removed
1 tablespoon olive oil
8 ounces white mushrooms, wiped clean and thinly sliced
4 ounces fresh goat cheese, crumbled
$1/2$ teaspoon sea salt
Freshly ground black pepper, to taste
1 tablespoon finely chopped cilantro
1 tablespoon finely chopped chives, plus 10 whole chives for tying the purses

In a blender, combine the eggs, flour, milk, water, salt, and butter and blend until smooth. Cover the container tightly and refrigerate the batter for at least 2 and up to 24 hours.

In a small bowl, whisk together the sour cream, cilantro, salt, and cumin. Whisk in enough of the water to make a smooth, creamy sauce. Cover with plastic wrap and refrigerate until serving time.

If the batter has separated, blend for a few seconds to recombine. The batter should be the consistency of thick cream; thin with a little additional milk, if necessary. Brush (or spray) a 6- or 7-inch nonstick or well-seasoned

*Continued over*

# Sausage and Fresh Goat Cheese Purses

cast-iron skillet with a little vegetable oil and heat over medium heat. Pour in about $1/4$ cup of the crêpe mixture and immediately swirl it all around so that the batter covers the entire base of the pan in a thin film, then quickly pour the rest back into the blender before it has a chance to set. Cook until the bottom is dappled brown, loosening the edges of the crêpe with a spatula. Flip the crêpe and cook for about 30 seconds more on the other side. When both sides are dappled brown, slide the crêpe onto a plate and continue making crêpes in the same manner, brushing with additional oil as necessary. If desired, wrap the crêpes with plastic wrap and refrigerate for up to 24 hours before assembling the purses.

Heat a large nonstick or cast-iron skillet over medium heat. Add the sausage and cook, crumbling and separating the meat with a wooden spoon, until only just done through, about 8 minutes. Do not overcook or the sausage will be dry. Transfer the sausage meat to a paper towel-lined plate with a slotted spoon and wipe the skillet clean with a paper towel.

Over medium-high heat, add the olive oil and sauté the mushrooms until softened and dry, about 5 minutes. You may need to increase the heat toward the end of the cooking time to cook off the excess moisture.

In a bowl, combine the mushrooms, sausage meat, goat cheese, salt, pepper, cilantro, and chives.

In a small saucepan of boiling water, blanch the whole chives for 10 seconds and lay out to dry on a paper towel.

Using a 4- or 5-ounce ramekin as a mold, fit the first crêpe gently into the base of the mold, leaving the edges hanging over the side all around. Place about $1^1/2$ tablespoons of the filling in the bottom and draw the edges of the crêpe together into a bunch. Pick up and mold the parcel into a round in the palm of your hand, then gather and squeeze gently but firmly together about 1 inch below the top. Tie the purse closed with a blanched chive. Transfer to a baking sheet and repeat with the remaining crêpes and filling to make 16 purses. Cover with a towel and set aside for up to 1 hour, if desired.

Preheat the oven to 350°F. Remove the towel and heat the purses through for 10 minutes, then serve immediately on warmed appetizer plates, with a dollop of the sauce on the side.

# Chicken Sausage, Zucchini, and Pasta Frittata

**SERVES 10 TO 12**

Frittatas are a great way to use up leftovers: pasta, vegetables—you name it. Just be sure to break up the pasta if it has formed a big, hard lump, as leftover pasta tends to do. A frittata can be served slightly warm, at room temperature, or even cold. It makes a good hearty breakfast for a crowd, and is also great on a picnic: either wrap wedges of the frittata individually, or take the whole thing on a platter and slice it on-site.

1 pound fresh, mild, reduced-fat chicken sausage,
such as Jody Maroni's All-Chicken Bistro, casings removed
$^1/_4$ cup fine, dried bread crumbs
1 tablespoon olive oil
$^3/_4$ pound small firm zucchini, coarsely grated
2 large garlic cloves, minced
2 tablespoons dry white wine (optional)
2 tablespoons thinly sliced fresh basil leaves (chiffonade)
$^1/_2$ cup tubetti or macaroni, cooked,
drained and tossed with 1$^1/_2$ teaspoons olive oil
6 sun-dried tomato halves, soaked in very hot water for 20 minutes,
squeezed dry, and finely chopped
$^3/_4$ cup coarsely grated Pecorino Romano cheese
$^1/_2$ teaspoon sea salt
$^1/_4$ teaspoon freshly ground black pepper
9 large eggs
1 cup milk
2 teaspoons Dijon-style mustard

Place the sausage in a nonstick or cast-iron skillet and heat over medium-low heat. Cook, breaking up and separating the sausage meat with a wooden spoon, until the meat is only just cooked through and no trace of pink remains, about 6 minutes. Do not overcook or it will be dry. Remove the sausage with a slotted spoon and drain on paper towels.

Preheat the oven to 350°F. Oil a 9-inch springform pan and coat it evenly with the bread crumbs, shaking out the excess.

Discard any fat in the skillet and wipe it with a paper towel. Add the oil and heat over medium heat. Add the zucchini and sauté for 3 minutes, until dry and bright green. Add the garlic and cook for about 1 minute, until it releases its aroma. Add the wine, if using, and cook for a few minutes more, until it has evaporated. Stir in the basil.

Combine and toss together the cooked pasta, tomatoes, cheese, salt, and pepper.

Spoon the cooked sausage into the prepared pan in an even layer. Spoon a layer of the zucchini mixture over the sausage, and spoon an even layer of the pasta mixture over the top.

In a bowl, whisk together the eggs, milk, and mustard. Pour the egg mixture evenly over the ingredients, taking care not to disturb the layers. Cover with foil and bake for 30 minutes, then remove the foil and cook for about 40 minutes more, until golden-brown and just firm in the center. Cool on a rack for 20 minutes, then loosen the sides with a small knife. Place a platter upside down on top of the pan and invert it, giving a brisk downward thrust to help release the frittata.

# Corn and Yucatan Sausage Soufflé

**SERVES 6 TO 8**

Soufflés are not scary. Just follow the rules, which include not opening the oven during baking time, and you are guaranteed success. If you use a fresh sausage without added cilantro, add 1/4 cup of chopped fresh cilantro to the mixture with the sausage. Be aware that the soufflé will start to fall within minutes of coming out of the oven. This is one dish where diners should be sitting at the table *before* you remove it from the oven.

2 links (about 1/2 pound total) fresh, reduced-fat, southwestern-style chicken and duck sausages, preferably Jody Maroni's Yucatan Sausage with Cilantro & Beer, casings removed
4 1/2 tablespoons butter
2 tablespoons grated imported Parmesan cheese
4 green onions, white and light green parts only, finely chopped
3 tablespoons all-purpose flour
2 cups milk, or half milk and half low-fat, low-sodium chicken broth, simmering
4 large egg yolks
1/2 teaspoon sea salt
1/4 teaspoon ground white pepper
1/2 cup corn kernels (from about 1/2 ear corn)
1/2 cup grated Jack or Havarti cheese
6 large egg whites
Pinch of salt

Place the sausage in a nonstick or cast-iron skillet and heat over medium-low heat. Cook, breaking up and separating the sausage meat with a wooden spoon, until the meat is only just cooked through and no trace of pink remains, about 6 minutes. Do not overcook or it will be dry. Remove the sausage with a slotted spoon and drain on paper towels until needed.

Using 1/2 tablespoon of the butter, grease an 8-cup soufflé dish and sprinkle it with the Parmesan, shaking the dish so the cheese evenly coats the inside. Preheat the oven to 400°F and place the rack in the center position.

In a large saucepan, heat the remaining 4 tablespoons of butter over medium-low heat. Add the green onions and stir for 2 minutes, then stir in the flour. Cook the mixture, stirring constantly, for 2 minutes or until the butter and flour paste is frothy but not browned. Remove the pan from the heat and whisk in the hot milk. Return the pan to the heat, raise the heat to medium, and stir the mixture constantly with a wooden spoon until simmering and quite thick, about 5 minutes. Remove the pan from the heat and whisk in the egg yolks one by one, whisking well between each addition so the yolks do not scramble. Stir in the sausage, salt, pepper, corn, and cheese.

In a large, clean bowl, beat the egg whites with a pinch of salt until they form stiff peaks, but don't beat so long that they become grainy. Stir one fourth of the egg whites into the sausage mixture to lighten it, then gently fold in the remaining whites, being careful not to stir too much air out of the mixture. The mixture should be only just combined. Turn into the prepared soufflé dish and place in the oven. Immediately reduce the temperature to 375°F and bake the soufflé for 30 minutes, until well risen. Serve immediately.

# Huevos a la Flamenco

SERVES 6

This breakfast or brunch dish will wake you right up with its bright colors and rich, complex flavors. The asparagus and peppers surround bright, sunny baked eggs and the peas make little mountains in between. The flavor-packed sofrito provides a base, and when you serve with a large, flat spoon, each diner gets a little of everything with a perfect egg in the center.

## Sofrito:

2 links (about ¹/₂ pound total) fresh, reduced-fat chicken and fruit sausage, preferably Jody Maroni's Chicken Apple Sausage with Sherry, casings removed
2 tablespoons olive oil
¹/₂ small white onion, finely chopped
2 large garlic cloves, finely chopped
1 red bell pepper, roasted, peeled, and finely chopped
2 large tomatoes, peeled, seeded and finely chopped
¹/₃ cup water
1 tablespoon finely chopped fresh parsley
1 small bay leaf
1 teaspoon sea salt
¹/₄ teaspoon freshly ground black pepper

## Eggs:

6 large fresh eggs, preferably free-range
¹/₂ cup cooked peas
16 small asparagus spears, blanched for 5 minutes in boiling water
1 red bell pepper, roasted, peeled, and cut into ¹/₂-inch-wide strips
2 tablespoons dry sherry

Sprigs of fresh parsley, for garnish
Chunks of grilled country bread, for serving

To make the sofrito, heat a large nonstick or cast-iron skillet over medium heat. Add the sausage and cook, breaking up and separating the sausage meat with a wooden spoon, for about 5 to 7 minutes, or until no trace of pink remains. Do not overcook. With a slotted spoon, transfer the sausage to a double thickness of paper towels to drain. Pour off and discard any fat from the skillet and wipe it with a paper towel. Add the oil. Over medium heat, sauté the onion, garlic, and red pepper for 5 minutes, until the vegetables are softened but not browned. Add the tomatoes, water, parsley, bay leaf, salt, and pepper and bring the mixture to a simmer. Cook until the liquid has almost evaporated and the mixture is quite thick. Discard the bay leaf, stir in the cooked sausage, and set aside.

Preheat the oven to 400°F and lightly oil a 9-inch square or round ceramic or earthenware casserole with 2-inch-high sides. Spread the sofrito evenly in the base of the dish and break the eggs carefully, one at a time, in a circle on the top. Heap the peas in 3 or 4 mounds in between the eggs and arrange the asparagus and pepper strips as a sort of frame for the eggs. Sprinkle the top with the sherry and bake for 20 minutes, or until the eggs are done to your liking.

Garnish with a few parsley sprigs and serve at once, accompanied by chunks of grilled country bread.

# a soup,

*salads,* &

sandwiches

# Chicken Sausage Dumpling and Slippery Noodle Soup

SERVES 8

Wonton wrappers are widely sold and are usually about 3-inch squares. They come in packages of varying weights, but one packet will certainly be enough for the dumplings here (ideally about 4 per person, or 32 total). Peel off the approximate number of wrappers you will use and wrap the remaining wrappers tightly, then freeze for future use (otherwise they may dry out and become brittle).

8 cups rich chicken broth, preferably homemade
1-inch piece fresh ginger (optional)
2-inch piece lemongrass, tender core only (optional)
$1/4$ pound dried cellophane noodles (also called bean threads)
2 links (about $1/2$ pound) fresh, reduced-fat chicken sausage
with an Asian flavor, preferably Jody Maroni's Chinese Chicken
& Duck Sausage with Cashews & Sesame, casings removed
2 tablespoons finely chopped fresh cilantro, plus whole sprigs, for garnish
1 tablespoon Vietnamese fish sauce (Nuoc Mam)
1 tablespoon low-sodium soy sauce
$1/4$ teaspoon granulated sugar
4 green onions, white and light green parts only, sliced paper-thin
1 package fresh wonton wrappers
1 egg, well beaten with a pinch of sea salt

If desired, simmer the broth for 15 minutes with the ginger and lemongrass. Strain and reserve, discarding the ginger. Thinly slice the lemongrass and reserve it for garnish.

Break the noodles in half, then place them in a large bowl. Pour warm water over to cover and set aside to soften for 20 minutes while you make the dumplings.

Cook sausage in a large nonstick or cast-iron skillet over medium heat, crumbling thoroughly with a wooden spoon, for about 8 minutes, or until cooked through (do not overcook or it may be dry). Transfer the sausage meat with a slotted spoon to paper towels to drain briefly, then combine in a bowl with the chopped cilantro, fish sauce, soy sauce, sugar, and half the green onions. Toss to mix thoroughly. If the sausage meat is still in large chunks, you will need to break it up into small pieces by hand or with a fork, otherwise it may tear the delicate wonton wrappers.

Place a wonton wrapper on the work surface with one pointed end toward you. Brush the edges with a little of the beaten egg and place about 1 teaspoon of the filling in the center. Bring the top corner down to meet the bottom and press all the edges together firmly, easing out any air that may be inside the dumpling before sealing. Dab a little egg on the outside corners and bring them together to meet in the center, pressing firmly. Continue making dumplings until you have used all the filling (this quantity makes about 24 dumplings).

In a large, wide soup pot, Dutch oven, or sauté pan, bring the broth to a simmer. Add the dumplings and cook for 3 minutes. Drain the soaking noodles thoroughly in a colander and add to the soup with the sliced lemongrass, if using. Cook for one minute more, then ladle into deep soup bowls, making sure each one gets an equal number of dumplings. Garnish each with a little of the remaining green onion and a sprig of cilantro and serve immediately.

# Toulouse Garlic Sausage Salad with Corn, Watercress, and Bruschetta

SERVES 4

This is a light and crunchy, refreshing lunch or light dinner salad. Grill the bread and the sausages just before serving and, for an even lighter dish, serve 1/2 sausage per person —you'll still get that great flavor!

## Dressing:

1 1/2 tablespoons balsamic vinegar
1/2 teaspoon sea salt
8 grinds black pepper
1/4 cup walnut or olive oil

4 links (about 1 pound total) fresh, reduced-fat pork and garlic sausages, such as Jody Maroni's Toulouse Garlic
2 tablespoons butter or olive oil
1 medium shallot, finely chopped
2 cups corn kernels (cut from about 2 ears), thoroughly thawed, if frozen
4 thick slices fresh country French, Italian, or sourdough bread, toasted on the grill until slightly golden
1 garlic clove, peeled and halved crosswise
1 bunch watercress, tough stems removed, rinsed and dried
Thinly sliced strips of pimiento, for garnish

In a small bowl, whisk the vinegar, salt, and pepper together, then drizzle in the oil in a thin stream, whisking all the time until the mixture is emulsified. Set aside until serving time.

Precook and then grill or broil the sausages as directed on page 14. Set aside to drain on paper towels.

In a heavy skillet, melt the butter over medium heat. Add the shallot and cook for 1 minute, then add the corn and toss for 2 minutes more. Remove from the heat and let cool to room temperature.

Rub the toasted bread slices firmly with the cut ends of the garlic clove and place in the center of a dinner plate. Slice the sausages crosswise on a sharp diagonal, about 1/2-inch thick, and fan one sausage around the edge of each plate.

Sprinkle the corn over the bruschetta and the sausages and distribute the watercress evenly over the top. Drizzle the dressing sparingly over the salads and place a few strips of pimiento over the top. Serve immediately.

# Salad Niçoise with All-Chicken Bistro Sausage

### SERVES 4 TO 6

This pungent salad is redolent with the sunny, salty flavors of the Mediterranean. It makes a substantial lunch or a satisfying outdoor dinner for summer nights too hot for whipping up a full dinner. Salad Niçoise is a perennial favorite with the French and is finding more and more fans in America now that we are more comfortable with eating anchovies. For those who still maintain a fear of the powerful little fish, cut the quantity in half, but please don't leave them out altogether or it won't be an authentic Niçoise.

## Dressing:

3 tablespoons red wine vinegar
2 cloves garlic, very finely chopped
1 small shallot, finely chopped
$1/2$ teaspoon sea salt
Freshly ground black pepper, to taste
1 tablespoon Dijon-style mustard
$1/2$ cup extra-virgin olive oil
2 teaspoons finely chopped fresh parsley

3 to 4 links ($3/4$ to 1 pound total) fresh, reduced-fat mild chicken sausage, such as Jody Maroni's All-Chicken Bistro
8 to 12 golf-ball-sized new potatoes, scrubbed and quartered
$1/4$ pound fine French green beans or small string beans, trimmed
2 heads Boston, limestone, or Bibb lettuce, pale inner leaves only, washed and dried
8 to 12 anchovy fillets, gently rinsed, patted dry, and halved lengthwise
1 tablespoon capers, rinsed and drained
4 to 6 large eggs, hard-boiled, shelled, and quartered
$1/2$ cup Niçoise olives or other brine-cured black olives (optional)

In a small bowl, whisk together the vinegar, garlic, shallot, salt, pepper, and mustard. Whisk in the oil in a thin stream, whisking constantly until emulsified. Stir in the parsley and set aside.

Precook and then grill or broil the sausages as directed on pages 14 and 16. Drain on paper towels and slice into $3/4$-inch chunks.

Bring two saucepans of lightly salted water to a boil. In one, boil the potatoes for about 10 minutes, until tender but not mushy. Drain in a colander, then immediately toss with 2 tablespoons of the dressing.

In the other saucepan, boil the beans for 4 to 6 minutes, depending on their size. Drain and refresh under cold running water, then drain again and spread on paper towels to dry.

On a large platter or on individual salad plates, make a layer of the lettuce, torn into bite-sized pieces. Arrange the potatoes, reserved sausage chunks, anchovies, capers, hard-boiled eggs, and olives, if using, evenly over the lettuce. Arrange the beans around the edge of the platter or plates. Whisk the dressing again to emulsify, then spoon evenly over the salad(s). Serve immediately.

# Raw Mushroom Salad with Boudin Blanc, Lemon, and Herbs

SERVES 4

One of the lightest dishes in the book, this clean and slightly tart salad virtually qualifies as "spa" cuisine, as long as you use a reduced-fat sausage. There is something so satisfying about a perfect, white mushroom—please choose nice plump fresh ones for this dish.

## Dressing:

1/4 teaspoon sea salt
1/8 teaspoon freshly ground black pepper
1 teaspoon finely chopped fresh marjoram
Juice of 1 large lemon
6 tablespoons extra-virgin olive oil

4 to 6 cups poaching liquid (water, low-fat, low-sodium chicken broth, white wine, or a combination of the three)
2 links (about 1/2 pound total) fresh, reduced-fat mild white sausages (chicken, chicken and duck, or veal), such as Jody Maroni's Boudin Blanc
1 rib celery, trimmed and cut into small dice
1 tablespoon chopped fresh flat-leaf parsley
6 to 8 leaves fresh basil, finely chopped
1/2 tablespoon finely chopped fresh mint (optional)
8 ounces medium, firm white mushrooms, brushed clean
1 small bunch chives, cut into 1-inch lengths
Coarsely cracked black pepper, to taste

In a small bowl, whisk together the salt, pepper, marjoram, and lemon juice. Whisk in the oil slowly, until the dressing is emulsified.

Bring the poaching liquid to a slow simmer in a medium saucepan (there should be enough liquid to cover the sausages by 3/4 inch). Add the sausages and simmer for about 6 minutes, until firm and cooked through. Do not overcook or they will be dry. When cool enough to handle, slice the sausages 3/4-inch thick and quarter the slices crosswise.

In a bowl, combine the celery, parsley, basil, and mint, if using, and toss to combine.

Just before serving, slice the mushrooms 1/4-inch thick. Arrange them in concentric circles on each of 4 plates, leaving a circle in the middle for the sausages.

Place a mound of sausages in the center of each plate and scatter the celery and herb mixture over the salads. Drizzle the dressing sparingly back and forth, and scatter the chives over the top. Season with coarsely cracked pepper to taste and serve immediately.

# Grilled Sausage Salad with Dandelion Greens and Fresh Goat Cheese

Dandelion greens are at their most tender in April and May, but are generally available year round. Larger greens tend toward the fibrous and bitter, so for this salad, try to find the small, pale, and crisp greens. The sugar in the dressing tames the tartness of the greens and intensifies the complex flavor of the sherry vinegar.

**5 to 7 cups poaching liquid (water, chicken broth, vegetable broth, white wine, or a combination)**
**3 links (about $3/4$ pound total) fresh, reduced-fat, slightly spicy poultry sausage, such as Jody Maroni's Orange-Garlic-Cumin Chicken & Duck**
**$3/4$ pound tender dandelion greens, washed and dried, woody stems discarded**
**$1/4$ pound fresh mild goat cheese, crumbled**
**2 tablespoons finely diced red onion**
**$2/3$ cup walnut or olive oil, or a combination**
**$1/3$ cup sherry vinegar**
**2 small garlic cloves, minced**
**1 teaspoon sugar**
**$1/2$ teaspoon sea salt**
**$1/4$ teaspoon freshly ground black pepper**

Bring the poaching liquid to a slow simmer in a large saucepan (there should be enough liquid to cover the sausages by $1/2$ inch). Add the sausages and poach for 4 minutes, then drain on paper towels. When the sausages are cool enough to handle, use a very sharp knife to slice them about $1/2$-inch thick.

Preheat a griddle or broiler until hot. Grill the sausage slices for 2 minutes, turning over halfway through, until browned and crisp. Drain on paper towels and cut them in half crosswise.

Cut the dandelion greens into 2-inch pieces and arrange on a large platter or individual serving plates. Scatter the sausage, goat cheese, and onion evenly over the top.

In a small saucepan, combine the oil, vinegar, garlic, sugar, salt, and pepper. Bring to a boil, whisking with a fork, and immediately drizzle over the salad. Toss the salad gently and serve immediately.

# New Orleans Oyster and Sausage Po'Boy

SERVES 4

Contrary to most people's expectations, the famous "po'boy" sandwich of New Orleans was not named after a poor, starving young lad, but rather after the French word *pourboire*, meaning "a tip." *Pourboire* translates literally as "for a drink," which is what most British people still say when they hand over a tip for services rendered. This is a rich and satisfying sandwich which must be eaten warm—for less ravenous appetites it would easily serve six.

1 long loaf very fresh French bread (about 1 1/4 pounds)
2 links (about 1/2 pound total) fresh, reduced-fat spicy pork or pork and beef sausages, such as Jody Maroni's Louisiana Boudin Hot Links, sliced about 3/4 inch thick
1 cup fine yellow cornmeal
1/4 teaspoon sea salt
1/4 teaspoon freshly ground black pepper
Pinch cayenne pepper
1/2 pint small oysters (approximately 18 to 26 per pint)
3 tablespoons peanut oil
1/4 head iceberg lettuce, shredded
1 ripe plum tomato, cored and sliced paper-thin
1 lemon, quartered
2 tablespoons mayonnaise, thinned with 2 teaspoons lemon juice

Split the loaf of French bread lengthwise and hollow the cut sides slightly, saving the crumbs for another use. Toast flat in the hot oven until the edges are only just golden, and set aside.

In a large, heavy cast-iron or nonstick skillet, place the slices of sausage cut side down and turn the heat to medium. Cook gently for 8 to 10 minutes, turning once halfway through the cooking time. Regulate the heat so the slices sizzle and brown but do not burn. Do not overcook or the sausage will be dry.

With a slotted spoon, remove the sausage slices from the pan and drain on paper towels, loosely tented with foil to keep them warm. Leave the pan on the stove.

In a large shallow bowl, combine the cornmeal, salt, pepper, and cayenne and toss together. Dredge the oysters thoroughly in the cornmeal mixture. Add the peanut oil to the same skillet and heat over medium heat until you see a haze over the oil. Throw a few grains of cornmeal into the oil to check the temperature— when the oil is hot enough the cornmeal should sizzle immediately. Fry the oysters for 3 minutes on each side, turning them gently with a flat-ended metal spatula so you can save the crust if it should stick a little bit. The oysters should be golden brown and almost firm. Immediately pile the oysters and the sausage into the bottom of the hollowed out loaf and top with the shredded lettuce. Overlap the sliced tomato all along the top. Squeeze a little lemon juice along the length of the sandwich, spread the top half of the bread with the mayonnaise, and place it firmly on top of the base. Cut the sandwich into 4 equal slices on the diagonal and serve at once.

# Eggplant and Garlic Sausage Sandwich with Curry Mayonnaise

SERVES 2

What can you do with a leftover sausage from the weekend barbecue? This exotic open-faced sandwich superbly combines the complementary flavors of curry mayonnaise and barbecue sauce, and seems about as far removed from "leftovers" as you can get. If you have more than one cooked sausage, just double the recipe to serve 4.

$1/2$ medium eggplant, cut lengthwise into $1/4$-inch thick slices
1 tablespoon olive oil
$1/4$ teaspoon sea salt
4 grinds of black pepper
2 thick slices country-style French, Italian, or sourdough bread
3 tablespoons mayonnaise, whisked together with $1/2$ teaspoon curry powder
1 precooked fresh, reduced-fat garlic-flavored sausage,
such as Jody Maroni's Toulouse Garlic, sliced $1/4$-inch thick
2 large slices fresh mozzarella (optional)
1 cup baby arugula leaves
2 tablespoons bottled barbecue sauce

Heat a well-seasoned ridged cast-iron griddle over medium-high heat. Brush the eggplant lightly with oil and season with the salt and pepper. Grill for 3 to 4 minutes, until tender and marked with the ridges of the griddle pan. Drain on paper towels. Grill the bread on both sides until just slightly toasted.

Place each slice of bread on a plate and spread the uppermost side with some of the curry mayonnaise, reserving a little for garnish. Top with sausage and a large slice of eggplant. If desired, top the eggplant with mozzarella. Scatter arugula leaves over the top of the sandwiches and on the plate. Drizzle barbecue sauce across the sandwich and add a dollop of the remaining curry mayonnaise in the center. This sandwich must be eaten with a knife and fork!

pastas, pizza, & calzone

# Penne with Chicken-Italian Sausage, Oven-Roasted Tomatoes, and Swiss Chard

SERVES 6

The slightly bitter Swiss chard and smoky, roasted tomatoes make a perfect foil for the rich and satisfying sausage in this dish. Without the rendered sausage fat and with only 1 tablespoon olive oil in the sauce, this dish is very low in fat—though it still tastes plenty satisfying. For those with nothing to fear, enrich the sauce with a little butter to add another layer of flavor.

Note: If you have any leftovers, use them to make the pasta frittata on page 55.

### Oven-roasted Tomatoes:

2 tablespoons extra-virgin olive oil
1 1/2 pounds plum tomatoes, stem ends removed, cut in half and seeds scraped out
Sea salt and freshly ground black pepper

### Chard and Sausage Sauce:

1 pound Swiss chard
1 1/4 pounds fresh, reduced-fat Mediterranean-flavored pork sausage, such as Jody Maroni's Pumante with Sun-dried Tomatoes & Prosciutto, sliced 3/4-inch thick
1 tablespoon olive oil
1 medium-size onion, finely chopped
1 small carrot, finely chopped
5 leaves fresh sage, finely chopped
2 garlic cloves, finely chopped

1 cup dry white wine
2 tablespoons tomato paste
1/2 teaspoon sea salt
1/4 teaspoon freshly ground black pepper

2 1/4 teaspoons coarse sea salt
1 pound best-quality imported penne
2 tablespoons unsalted butter, cut into 4 pieces (optional)
1/4 teaspoon freshly ground black pepper

Preheat the oven to 200°F. Brush a large baking sheet with oil and lay the tomatoes on it in a single layer, cut side up. Sprinkle them with salt and pepper, then turn cut side down. Brush the skin side of the tomatoes with oil and sprinkle with salt and pepper. Roast for 4 to 6 hours, regulating the heat so it doesn't get so hot that the tomatoes burn. Prop the oven open by 1 inch with a dish towel if the temperature is difficult to regulate at such a low heat. The tomatoes are done when they are shrunken, dehydrated, and shriveled on top but still quite juicy underneath. Cool on the baking sheet. Cut in half lengthwise and then again crosswise. Cover with plastic wrap until needed.

Rinse and drain the chard. Remove the leaves from the ribs; trim and discard the woody bottoms. Finely chop the ribs, coarsely chop the leaves, and set both aside separately.

In a large, well-seasoned cast-iron or nonstick skillet, cook the sausages over medium-low heat for about 6 minutes, stirring occasionally, until no trace of pink remains. With a slotted spoon, remove them to a double thickness of paper towels to drain briefly. Discard the fat from the pan and wipe with a paper towel. Add the oil and, over medium heat, sauté the onion and carrot for 6 to 8 minutes, or until the onion is translucent. Return the sausage to the pan, add the sage and garlic, and stir for 2 minutes. Add half the wine and half the tomato paste and stir until most of the wine has evaporated. Add the oven-roasted tomatoes, chopped chard ribs, remaining wine, remaining tomato paste, salt, and pepper. Cover the pan and cook, stirring occasionally, for 10 minutes. Remove from the heat, cover, and set aside while you cook the pasta, or for up to 1 hour.

In a large saucepan, bring a generous amount of water to a boil and add 2 teaspoons of the salt. Add the penne and cook for about 13 minutes, or until al dente.

While the pasta is cooking, return the sauce to medium-high heat, add the chard leaves, and cover. After 2 minutes, remove the lid and stir to mix. Repeat twice more and, after about 6 minutes when the chard leaves have melted into the sauce, remove from the heat. Taste for seasoning and, if desired, stir in the butter until it is absorbed. Drain the pasta well and toss it with the remaining 1/4 teaspoon salt and the pepper. Mound some penne into each of 6 heated shallow bowls and spoon the sauce evenly over the top.

# Fusilli with Red Wine-Braised Sausage and Carrots

SERVES 4 TO 6

This is a perfect dish for early fall, when it's cold enough outside to make you hungry for a warm, comforting, one-pot meal. It's also the season for ripe, flavorful tomatoes, so by all means substitute 4 or 5 peeled, seeded, and chopped fresh plum tomatoes for the canned ones called for below. The zucchini adds a welcome bright green, fresh, and crisp note to this extra-satisfying dish with its roots firmly planted in the Italian countryside.

4 links (about 1 pound total) fresh,
reduced-fat mild Italian pork sausage, casings removed
1 tablespoon olive oil
1 large onion, coarsely chopped
1 medium carrot, chopped into 1/4-inch chunks
2 cloves garlic, finely chopped
1 tablespoon finely chopped fresh sage
1 1/2 tablespoons tomato paste
Sea salt
Freshly ground black pepper, to taste
1 3/4 cups hearty red wine
1 pound dried fusilli pasta, preferably imported
1 (14-ounce) can peeled chopped tomatoes, with their liquid
1 medium zucchini, quartered lengthwise
1 cup grated imported Parmesan cheese

In a very large heavy sauté pan or skillet, cook the sausages over medium-low heat for about 8 minutes, stirring occasionally and breaking up with a wooden spoon. With a slotted spoon, transfer the sausage meat to a double thickness of paper towels to drain. Pour off and discard most of the fat from the pan, leaving behind a thin film and all the little browned bits of sausage that remain.

Add the oil and, over medium heat sauté the onion and two-thirds of the carrot together, stirring occasionally until slightly golden, about 10 minutes (be careful not to let the mixture burn). Add the garlic and the sage and cook for about 1 minute more, than add the sausage, tomato paste, 1/2 teaspoon salt, pepper, and half the wine. Control the heat so that the mixture simmers actively. Stir frequently, so the mixture does not stick to the pan, and reduce until most of the wine has evaporated. Add the remaining wine and remaining chopped carrot, partially cover the pan and cook over low heat for about 12 minutes more, until very thick and saucy. (At this point you could cover the sauce and set it aside for up to 1 hour before gently reheating and continuing with the recipe.)

While the sauce cooks, bring a generous amount of water to the boil in a large saucepan and add 1 tablespoon salt. Add the fusilli to the boiling water and at the same time add the tomatoes and the zucchini to the sauce. Cook the pasta until al dente, according to the package instructions. Stir the gently simmering sauce while the pasta cooks and taste for seasoning.

Drain the pasta and add it to the pan with the sauce. Add about 1/2 cup of the Parmesan, or to taste, and toss to coat the pasta evenly. Serve in warmed, large shallow bowls and pass the remaining Parmesan at the table.

# Capellini with Oysters, White Wine, Spicy Sausage, and Watercress

SERVES 6

This dish is quite a revelation—you might never imagine that these unusual ingredients would go so well together. It's a delicate, slightly elegant presentation, with a serious but not overwhelming kick provided by the spicy sausage. Be sure to plan the final assembly carefully, as there is nothing worse than an overcooked oyster!

5 to 7 cups poaching liquid (water, broth, beer, white wine, or a combination)
3 links (about $3/4$ pound total) fresh, reduced-fat spicy pork sausage, such as Jody Maroni's Louisiana Boudin Hot Links
1 tablespoon coarse sea salt
1 tablespoon butter
2 large shallots, minced
$1^{1}/_{2}$ cups low-fat, low-sodium chicken broth
1 sprig fresh thyme
1 pound dried imported capellini
$2/_{3}$ cup heavy cream
1 pint small shucked oysters, with their liquor (if the oysters are large, halve or quarter them)
1 tablespoon finely chopped fresh parsley
Freshly ground white pepper, to taste
1 small bunch watercress, tender leaves and stems only, finely chopped
6 sprigs of watercress, for garnish

Bring the poaching liquid to a slow simmer in a large saucepan (the liquid should cover the sausages by $1/_{2}$ inch). Add the sausages and poach them for 4 minutes, then drain on paper towels. When they are cool enough to handle, use a very sharp knife to cut them into slices about $1/_{2}$-inch thick.

Preheat a griddle, a large cast-iron skillet, or the broiler until hot. Grill the sausage slices for 2 minutes, turning them over halfway through, until brown and crisp. Drain on paper towels and cut them into halves, so that they are about the size of the oysters. Set aside.

Bring a large pot of water to a boil and add the salt. Warm 6 serving plates in a low oven.

When the water is about to boil, melt the butter in a very large sauté pan over medium-low heat. Add the shallots and sauté, stirring, for about 5 minutes, until they are softened. Add the broth and thyme and raise the heat to medium-high. When the broth is simmering, add the capellini to the boiling water and, at the same time, stir the cream, oysters with their liquor, parsley, and pepper into the broth. Cook both the sauce and the pasta for about 3 minutes, then quickly drain the pasta and add it to the sauce along with the reserved sausage and the chopped watercress. Reduce the heat to low and toss the mixture with tongs just until the pasta is evenly coated and heated through; do not overcook or the oysters will be tough. Garnish with sprigs of watercress and serve immediately.

# Little Duck Sausage Pizzas with Fennel and Smoked Mozzarella

SERVES 6

Pizza dough is now available in many supermarkets and Italian delicatessens, and almost any bakery will be happy to sell you a lump of raw bread dough, which is the same thing. Make sure the dough is at or near room temperature before starting to work with it or it will fight back hard at every step.

These flavors are very *nuovo Italiano*, and would make a great large pizza as well. Be careful—their small size makes them very tempting, and they're likely to disappear before you've even tried one.

1½ tablespoons olive oil
1 fennel bulb, trimmed, cut in half lengthwise, cored and thinly sliced
1 medium-size sweet onion, coarsely chopped
1 tablespoon finely chopped fresh thyme, or 1 teaspoon dried thyme, crumbled
½ teaspoon sea salt
Freshly ground black pepper
1 link (about 4 ounces) fresh, reduced-fat fennel-flavored duck sausage, such as Jody Maroni's All-Duck with Fennel, Coriander, & Sage, casing removed
1 pound homemade or store-bought pizza dough
8 Italian oil-cured black olives, pitted and quartered
4 ounces smoked mozzarella, sliced and torn into small pieces
Wedge of imported Parmesan cheese, for shaving
Small handful fresh cilantro leaves
Small handful fresh flat-leaf parsley leaves

In a medium-size skillet, heat the oil over low heat. Add the fennel and onion and cook slowly for 20 to 25 minutes, or until very soft and slightly caramelized. Stir in the thyme, salt, and ¼ teaspoon pepper, and remove the pan from the heat. Heat a heavy cast-iron or non-stick skillet over medium-low heat. Add the sausage and cook, stirring and breaking up the sausage meat with a spoon, until no trace of pink remains, 5 to 7 minutes. With a slotted spoon, transfer the sausage meat to a double layer of paper towels to drain (at this stage you could cool both the fennel mixture and the sausage meat and refrigerate them for several hours; they do not need to be reheated before topping the pizza).

Preheat the oven to 450°F. Cut the pizza dough into 6 equal balls. Place the dough balls on a large, lightly oiled baking sheet, cover with a towel, and allow to rest for 15 minutes. With your fingertips, press each ball out into a 4-inch round.

Poke the olives into the tops of the pizzas and spread an equal amount of the fennel-onion mixture onto each one, leaving a ¼-inch border. Crumble some of the cooked sausage over the top of each pizza and sprinkle with the mozzarella. Season with pepper, to taste.

Bake for 10 to 12 minutes, or until the edges are golden and the mozzarella has melted. Shave a few curls of Parmesan over the top and sprinkle with a few cilantro and parsley leaves. Serve immediately.

# Pizza Rustica

In New York's Little Italy, pizza rustica holds pride of place in the windows of the very best corner grocers. Studded with sausage and bright red peppers and encased in a golden pastry case, this is the ultimate in picnic food. Assembling it may take a little time, but the flavor actually improves after a day of refrigeration, so there is no need for a last-minute rush. Be sure to return to room temperature before serving, though, to fully appreciate all of the flavors.

## Pastry shell:

3 cups all-purpose flour
1 tablespoon sugar
$1/2$ teaspoon sea salt
6 ounces cold unsalted butter, cut into about 20 pieces
3 large egg yolks, lightly beaten
$1/4$ cup plus 1 tablespoon ice water

## Filling:

2 links (about $1/2$ pound total) fresh,
hot Italian sausage, casings removed
2 links (about $1/2$ pound total) fresh,
sweet Italian sausage, casings removed
4 large eggs, lightly beaten
$2 1/2$ cups ricotta cheese
1 pound spinach leaves,
blanched for 2 minutes in boiling water and squeezed dry
3 roasted red bell peppers (available in jars),
cut into 1-inch pieces (about 1 cup)
2 ounces prosciutto, excess fat discarded, finely chopped
$1/4$ cup grated imported Parmesan or Romano cheese
1 teaspoon sea salt
Freshly ground black pepper, to taste
Dash of nutmeg
$1/4$ pound imported Italian fontina cheese, cut into $1/2$-inch dice
1 large egg beaten with 1 tablespoon milk

*Continued over*

In a food processor, combine the flour, sugar, and salt and process just to blend. Remove the cover and scatter the pieces of butter over the top. Pulse on and off a few times for 2 or 3 seconds each, until the butter is the size of peas. Remove the cover, and drizzle the yolks and $1/4$ cup of the ice water over the top. Pulse again 3 or 4 times, until the dough starts to come together and form several large clumps. If the dough does not come together almost immediately, add 1 or 2 tablespoons of ice water. Scrape down the bowl once, and avoid overprocessing or the dough will be tough. Turn out onto a lightly floured surface and shape quickly into a rough ball. Cut off about one third of the dough and roll both pieces into round, flattened disks. Wrap each tightly with plastic wrap and refriger-

ate for at least 1 hour and up to 8 hours.

Heat a large nonstick or cast-iron skillet over medium-low heat. Add the sausage and cook, crumbling and separating the meat with a wooden spoon, until only just cooked through, about 7 minutes. Do not overcook or the sausage will be dry. With a slotted spoon, transfer the sausage meat to a double layer of paper towels to drain and cool.

In a large bowl, combine the eggs and ricotta and mix well. Coarsely chop the spinach and add it to the egg mixture. Add the crumbled sausage meat, red peppers, prosciutto, Parmesan, salt, pepper, and nutmeg. Fold in the fontina cheese.

Preheat the oven to 375°F. On a lightly floured surface, roll out the larger piece of dough to a round about 16 inches in diameter and $1/8$-inch thick. Ease the dough down into a 9-inch springform pan, gently pushing it into the corners without stretching or tearing the dough. Trim the edges of the dough with scissors, leaving a 1-inch overhang. Mound the filling mixture into the pastry case and spread it evenly, smoothing the top. Quickly roll out the smaller piece of pastry to a round about 1 inch larger than the top of the pan. Brush the edges of the lower pastry overhang with the egg wash and fit the pastry top over, matching the edges. Crimp the edges together with a fork, sealing firmly and making an attractive pattern. Trim the pastry with scissors so that the edges are exactly even. Slash the top of the pastry in 2 or 3 places and brush the top with egg wash. Bake on the center rack of the oven for 1 hour and 15 minutes. The top should be deep golden-brown. Transfer the pan to a rack to cool for at least 30 minutes before unmolding onto a platter. Serve warm, cut into wedges or cover and refrigerate for up to 2 days before serving at room temperature or slightly warmed in a low oven. Do not serve cold or much of the flavor will be lost.

# Artichoke, Fontina, and Garlic Sausage Calzone

MAKES 2 LARGE CALZONE, SERVES 4 TO 6

If you are an aficionado of making your own pizza dough, it will give you the best result with this dish. However, most bakeries will sell you a lump of uncooked, risen white bread dough (which is all pizza dough is) if you ask them nicely. Otherwise, many stores now sell pop-out pizza in the same tubes that muffins have come in since antiquity. Just don't try to reroll such dough into a round because believe me, it doesn't want to change. Stay with the square shape and fold it over into a rectangular calzone. Plural and singular of calzone are the same word, so don't be confused by "Place the calzone in the oven." I *do* mean both of them.

1½ pounds homemade or store-bought pizza dough, at room temperature
2 links (about ½ pound) fresh, reduced-fat garlic-flavored sausages, such as Jody Maroni's Toulouse Garlic, casings removed
¾ cup drained and coarsely chopped marinated artichoke hearts
¼ cup grated imported Parmesan cheese
Sea salt and freshly ground black pepper, to taste
10 leaves fresh basil, torn into small pieces (optional)
3 ounces imported Italian fontina or smoked mozzarella, or a mixture of both, thinly sliced
¾ cup good-quality bottled tomato sauce
Olive oil, for brushing calzone

Divide the dough into 2 equal pieces and roll each into a smooth ball. Let rest, covered with a towel, for 20 minutes at room temperature to relax the dough.

Flatten each dough ball with the palm of your hand and then press out to a 7-inch round with your fingertips. Cover the rounds with a towel.

If using store-bought pizza dough, press out according to the package instructions into two rounds or, with some products, two squares.

In a nonstick or cast-iron skillet, cook the sausage over medium-low heat for 6 to 8 minutes, until cooked through, breaking up the meat with a wooden spoon. Do not overcook or it will be dry. With a slotted spoon, transfer the crumbled sausage to a paper towel-lined plate to drain.

Preheat the oven to 425°F.

Place half the chopped artichokes on the half of the dough round closest to you. Top with half of the sausage and Parmesan, salt, pepper, and half the basil, if using. Lay half the sliced cheese over the top. Leave a generous border, but make sure the filling isn't mounded too high in the center. It should evenly cover the half-round (or half-square). Drizzle 1 tablespoon of the tomato sauce over the filling and brush the edges with a little water. Gently fold the top half of the dough round towards you to cover the filling, so that the 2 edges meet. Seal the edges by firmly pinching and crimping, making sure they are well-sealed. Repeat the process for the remaining calzone. Brush the tops of each calzone with a little oil and transfer them to a baking sheet with a large spatula.

Bake the calzone for about 20 minutes, until crisp and golden. Warm the remaining tomato sauce and cut the calzone into halves or one-third wedges. Serve immediately.

# ONE

**pot** meals

everything else

# Portuguese Bean Stew with Chicken and Turkey Chorizo

### SERVES 6 TO 8

The Portuguese love to combine kale and sausages, and it's always been one of my favorite duos, too. Whether it's a grilled sausage with sautéed garlic and kale, a sausage and kale soup, or this comforting stew, it's definitely a winning combination.

4 links (about 1 pound total) fresh chorizo-style sausage, such as Jody Maroni's Chicken & Turkey Chorizo
2 tablespoons olive oil
1 large yellow onion, coarsely chopped
4 large garlic cloves, finely chopped
3 medium white or Red Rose (boiling) potatoes, peeled, and cut into $1/2$-inch dice
1 pound kale, tough stems cut away and discarded, coarsely chopped
$2 1/2$ cups cooked red kidney beans (or use good quality canned beans, well-rinsed and drained)
2 cups low-fat, low-sodium chicken broth
1 cup water
1 cup dry white wine
2 sprigs of fresh mint
1 bay leaf
$1/2$ teaspoon sea salt
$1/8$ teaspoon cayenne pepper

Place the sausages and $1/2$ cup water in a large, heavy skillet. Cook over medium-high heat for about 10 minutes, turning the sausages occasionally, until the water has evaporated. Reduce the heat to low and cook for about 5 minutes more, turning the sausages until they are nicely browned. When cool enough to handle, slice $1/2$-inch thick.

In a large covered casserole, heat the oil over medium heat. Add the onion and cook, stirring, for about 7 minutes, until softened. Add the garlic and cook for 1 minute more. Add the potatoes and kale and cover. Stir occasionally for about 5 minutes, until the potatoes are slightly golden and the kale is wilted. Add the reserved sausages, beans, broth, water, wine, mint, bay leaf, salt, and cayenne. Slowly simmer, partially covered, for about $1 1/2$ to 2 hours, until the potatoes are tender. If the stew is too soupy, increase the heat to medium-high, remove the lid, and reduce a little to a stew-like consistency. Serve in warm shallow bowls.

# Choucroute Garnie with Garlic and Chicken Bistro Sausages

SERVES 6 TO 8

I like using smoked bacon for this dish, since the smoky flavor goes perfectly with the crisp sauerkraut, but if you can't find it, regular bacon is fine. Rinse the sauerkraut thoroughly, as its saltiness can be overwhelming. If you use fresh sauerkraut, the cooking time will be between 2 and 3 hours and the liquid should be increased by about half.

Note: Ask your butcher to cut the smoked turkey up for you, or use a good heavy cleaver helped along by a wooden meat mallet (it takes several really strong whacks to get through the turkey bones).

3 pounds sauerkraut, preferably in a bag
6 to 8 cups poaching liquid (water, beer, broth, or a combination)
2 links (about $1/2$ pound total) fresh, garlic-flavored reduced-fat pork sausages, such as Jody Maroni's Toulouse Garlic
2 links (about $1/2$ pound total) fresh, reduced-fat chicken sausage, such as Jody Maroni's All-Chicken Bistro with Roasted Garlic & Rosemary
2 slices bacon, preferably smoked, cut crosswise into thin strips
Olive or vegetable oil
1 medium-size onion, thinly sliced
$1^{1}/_{2}$ Granny Smith or other tart apples, peeled, cored, and diced
$1/2$ teaspoon sea salt
$1/4$ teaspoon freshly ground black pepper
1 medium carrot, finely diced
1 bay leaf
1 sprig each fresh thyme and parsley
2 cups light chicken broth, preferably homemade
$1^{1}/_{2}$ cups Riesling, Gewürztraminer, or other slightly sweet white wine
3 tablespoons gin or 5 juniper berries tied inside a cheesecloth bag
$1^{1}/_{2}$ pounds smoked turkey pieces, cut into 2- or 3-inch chunks
$1/2$ teaspoon caraway seeds

In a large bowl of cold water, soak the sauerkraut for 1 hour, draining and rinsing thoroughly in 2 or 3 changes of water. Drain again and squeeze dry.

In a large saucepan, bring the poaching liquid to a simmer (there should be enough liquid to cover the sausages by $1/2$ inch). Poach the sausages for about 6 minutes (do not overcook or they will be dry). Reserve 2 cups of the poaching liquid. When cool enough to handle, slice the sausages into 2-inch lengths on a diagonal and set aside.

Preheat the oven to 350°F.

In a large, flameproof covered casserole, sauté the bacon over low heat until most of the fat is rendered out. Transfer the bacon to a paper towel to drain. Discard all but 1 tablespoon of the fat from the pan, or add enough olive or vegetable oil to the bacon drippings to make 1 tablespoon. Add the onion and sauté, stirring occasionally, for about 10 minutes, or until softened but not browned. Add the apples, salt, and pepper and cook for 2 minutes more. Add the reserved bacon, sauerkraut, carrot, bay leaf, thyme and parsley. Pour the reserved poaching liquid, broth, wine, and gin over the top (the liquid should almost but not quite cover the sauerkraut). Nestle the sausage pieces and turkey in the sauerkraut and scatter the caraway seeds over the top. Cover and bake for about 1 hour, until nice and juicy. Discard the bay leaf and herb sprigs, and serve in large shallow bowls.

# Grilled Skewers of Sausage, Apples, Bay Leaves, and Country Bread

SERVES 6

If you don't have metal skewers, long bamboo skewers work fine as long as you remember to soak them in water for at least 2 hours before threading and grilling—otherwise they have a nasty tendency to catch fire at the end, just where you were about to pick them up.

Do be sure to watch the bread: as soon as it begins to char, it's time to grab these skewers off the fire and throw them onto your favorite platter. It is best to assemble all the prepared ingredients and begin threading the skewers about 10 minutes before the grilling fire will be ready.

6 fresh, reduced-fat mild pork or pork & beef sausage, such as Jody Maroni's Danziger Polish, about 4 ounces each
1 tart green apple, peeled, cored, and cut into 1-inch chunks
2 ounces thinly sliced pancetta or prosciutto, cut into approximately 5 x 1-inch strips
1/2 cup extra-virgin olive oil
1 tablespoon finely chopped fresh oregano or 1 teaspoon dried oregano, crumbled
1 teaspoon freshly ground black pepper
6 to 8 garlic cloves, finely chopped
20 (1-inch) cubes slightly stale country-style French, Italian, or sourdough bread
20 bay leaves, preferably fresh, or at least not too brittle (optional; fresh bay leaves are often available in good produce markets)
Sea salt and freshly ground black pepper, to taste
Lemon wedges, for garnish
Fresh oregano or parsley sprigs, for garnish (optional)

If using bamboo skewers, soak ten 8-inch skewers for at least 2 hours before you plan to grill.

Preheat the oven to 350°F. Prebake the sausages on a roasting rack for 15 to 20 minutes, until firm (see page 16). When cool enough to handle, slice into 1-inch lengths.

Wrap each apple chunk with a strip of pancetta, winding it around several times so that it will stay put.

In a bowl, whisk together the oil, oregano, pepper, and garlic. Toss the bread cubes in the marinade, making sure all sides are evenly coated, and leave in the marinade, tossing every few minutes, while you heat a covered outdoor grill, or a broiler to medium.

Thread the ingredients onto the skewers, alternating and putting an equal quantity of sausage, apple, bread, and bay leaves on each skewer. Season with salt and pepper.

Place the skewers on the hot grill and close the cover. After 2 minutes, use long handled tongs to turn to the other side. Grill, covered, for 2 minutes more then check and turn again. Cook only until the pancetta is crispy and the bread is deep golden, about 6 minutes. Immediately transfer to a platter and garnish with lemon wedges and fresh sprigs of oregano.

# Duck Sausage Jambalaya

SERVES 8 TO 10

More than virtually any other recipe in this book, Jambalaya is *the* classic sausage dish. Of course, as with any Southern dish, authoritative recipes abound, and it can be made with ham (the name actually originated from the French word for ham, *jambon*), chicken, or seafood. This is a good dish for feeding a crowd, and if unexpected guests arrive you can increase the amount of rice and stock to make the same basic ingredients feed many extra mouths.

1 1/2 pounds fresh, reduced-fat duck or chicken and duck sausage, such as Jody Maroni's Boudin Blanc, casings removed

1/4 pound fresh spicy chicken and turkey sausage, such as Jody Maroni's Chicken & Turkey Chorizo with Fresh Mint & Balsamic Vinegar, casings removed

1 tablespoon olive oil

1 medium-size yellow onion, coarsely chopped

1 large green pepper, cored, seeded, and diced

1 large red pepper, cored, seeded, and diced

4 garlic cloves, finely chopped

2 ribs celery, finely chopped

2 bay leaves

1 1/2 cups long-grain rice

2 cups chopped tomatoes, drained, or 8 plum tomatoes, peeled, seeded, and chopped

1/4 teaspoon cayenne pepper, or to taste

3 cups low-fat, low-sodium chicken broth, or half broth and half water

1 teaspoon sea salt

Freshly ground black pepper

8 green onions, white, light green, and crisp green parts only, thinly sliced

In a large flameproof casserole, cook the sausages over medium heat, stirring occasionally and breaking up with a wooden spoon, until almost no pink remains, 8 to 10 minutes. With a slotted spoon, transfer the sausage meat to paper towels to drain. Pour all the liquid from the pan into a glass measuring cup and let settle for 1 minute. Spoon off about 2 tablespoons of the bright red fat (it is red from the spices in the chorizo) and return it to the pan. Discard the remaining juices, and add the oil to the pan.

Add the onion, green pepper, red pepper, garlic, celery, and bay leaves to the pan and sauté over medium-low heat, stirring occasionally, until the vegetables are very soft and golden, about 15 minutes. Add the rice and stir until it is slightly golden, about 5 minutes. Add the tomatoes and cayenne pepper and stir for 2 minutes. Add the broth, reserved sausage mixture, salt, and pepper and bring the mixture to a simmer. Cover the dish and reduce the heat to very low. Simmer gently for 45 to 50 minutes, until the rice is tender and somewhat sticky. Check the pan occasionally to make sure the liquid has not completely evaporated and add 1/2 cup extra hot broth or water as necessary, so that the rice is moist and juicy but not wet. Remove the bay leaves and stir in half the green onions. Serve immediately, scattering the remaining green onions over each portion.

# Paella with Duck Sausage and Shrimp

**SERVES 8**

In Spain, paella is a celebration dish which can include any of the following ingredients: rabbit, clams, mussels, lobster, chicken, squid, cured sausage, air-dried ham, and snails. It was traditionally cooked (by men only!) over an outdoor fire made of driftwood or vine cuttings. This version is simpler but just as festive.

If you are tempted to experiment with making your own sausage (see page 92), this is one of the classic dishes to benefit from your efforts. Instead of tying off the sausage into links as usual, leave it in one continuous 1 1/2-pound sausage link. Then, curl it into a flat spiral and secure with two criss-crossed metal skewers to keep the sausage flat. Prebake as usual (see page 16), then grill for about 4 minutes over a hot fire, turning over halfway through. Set aside until the rice is almost ready and add to the dish, as below. It makes a really impressive "garnish" for this already gorgeous dish with its golden yellow, aromatic rice and pink, juicy shrimp.

If you have a large enough pan, this dish is perfect for feeding a crowd—I especially like to cook it outdoors on the barbecue, just as the Spanish cowboys and fishermen used to do.

1 pound jumbo shrimp, deveined (through the back of the shell if desired)
3 large garlic cloves, thickly sliced
1/4 cup extra-virgin olive oil
1 tablespoon finely chopped fresh parsley
Freshly ground black pepper, to taste
Dash of cayenne pepper, or to taste
2 tablespoons white wine or vermouth
1 tablespoon fresh lemon juice
6 to 8 cups poaching liquid (water, stock, wine, or a combination)
1 1/2 pounds fresh, reduced-fat duck sausage, such as Jody Maroni's All-Duck
with Fennel, Coriander, & Sage

*Continued over*

In a large bowl, combine the shrimp, garlic, oil, parsley, black pepper, cayenne, wine, and lemon juice. Cover and refrigerate for up to 2 hours.

In a large saucepan, bring the poaching liquid to a simmer (the liquid should cover the sausages by 1/2 inch). Simmer the sausages for about 8 minutes. Do not overcook or they will be dry. When cool enough to handle, slice the sausages into 2- or 3-inch lengths on the diagonal and set aside on paper towels.

For the rice, in a small saucepan or a microwave, heat the wine until hot. Place the saffron threads in a small bowl, add the hot wine, and set aside for at least 15 minutes.

In a medium saucepan, combine the broth, fish stock, and water and bring to a boil.

Drain the shrimp from their marinade; pick out and discard the garlic.

In a very large, heavy skillet or paella pan (about 18 inches is ideal), heat the olive oil over medium-high heat. Sauté the shrimp for about 2 minutes, tossing and stirring frequently. With a slotted spoon, transfer the shrimp to a plate, draining as much oil as possible back into the pan. Reduce the heat to medium-low. Sauté the onion for about 5 minutes, stirring occasionally, until softened. Add the rice and the saffron-wine mixture to the pan and stir for about 5 minutes, or until the rice is translucent. Season with salt and pepper and add the boiling broth mixture. Jiggle the pan carefully to help the rice find its level, reduce the heat to low and cook the rice for 18 to 20 minutes. (Ideally, all the rice should be cooking at a very slow simmer, so rotate the pan and stir gently if necessary to ensure even cooking.) About 5 minutes before the rice will be done, stir the peas and green beans into the rice and nestle the sausages on the top. Tent the pan loosely with foil (or cover with a lid, if available). When the rice is just tender, distribute the red peppers and shrimp attractively over the top, cover again and continue cooking for about 2 minutes more, just to heat through. Remove from the heat and place lemon wedges all around the edges. Serve directly from the pan.

## Rice:

2 tablespoons white wine
1 generous teaspoon saffron threads
5 cups chicken broth, preferably homemade
2 cups fish stock or bottled clam juice
2 cups water
1/4 cup olive oil
1 large red onion, finely chopped
4 1/2 cups short-grain rice (Arborio is a good variety)
Sea salt and freshly ground black pepper, to taste
1 (10-ounce) package frozen baby peas,
thawed for 5 minutes in boiling water and drained
1/2 pound small green beans, trimmed and blanched
for 5 minutes in boiling water (optional)
2/3 cup wood-roasted red peppers (sold in a jar), cut into strips
3 large lemons, cut into wedges

# Roasted Pork Loin with Fig, Marsala, and Pine Nut Sausage Stuffing

SERVES 6 TO 8

An excellent and elegant special occasion dish, this luscious loin of pork with its colorful stuffing would make a marvelous centerpiece for a grand buffet table. Pork and fruit seem to have a great affinity for one another, and this dish takes advantage of the sweetness of dried fruits along with the delicate flavor of today's leaner cuts of pork (by the way, kids really seem to love these flavors!). Of course, you could substitute any good fresh sausage, but using Figs, Marsala, & Pine Nuts sausage makes a dish that's truly out of this world!

2 links (about $1/2$ pound total) fresh, reduced-fat, fruit-flavored pork sausage, such as Jody Maroni's Figs, Marsala, & Pine Nuts
4 ounces dried apricots
$1 1/4$ cups sherry
$1/2$ cup water
1 tablespoon olive oil
$1/2$ yellow onion, coarsely chopped
2 garlic cloves, minced
$1/2$ cup coarsely chopped fresh spinach (firmly packed)
Zest of one scrubbed orange, minced
$1/4$ cup pine nuts, toasted (omit if using J.M. Figs, Marsala, & Pine Nuts)
$3/4$ teaspoon sea salt
Freshly ground black pepper, to taste
1 large egg, lightly beaten
4- to 5-pound boneless pork loin, fat trimmed and with a long deep pocket cut into the length for the stuffing
$1/4$ cup Dijon-style mustard
$1/4$ cup orange marmalade

Steam the sausages for 15 minutes over gently simmering water. Drain briefly on paper towels, slice $1/2$-inch thick on the diagonal, and cut the slices crosswise in half. While the sausages are steaming, in a small saucepan, combine the apricots, 1 cup of the sherry, and the water and simmer, covered, for 10 minutes. Remove from the heat, cool, then chop coarsely. In a medium skillet, heat the oil over medium-low heat and sauté the onion and garlic for about 5 minutes, until softened. Add the spinach and cook for 3 minutes more, stirring, until the spinach has wilted. Cool.

In a large bowl, combine the sausages, apricots, onion mixture, orange zest, pine nuts, if using, salt, pepper, and egg. Combine thoroughly and refrigerate the stuffing until chilled, about 1 hour. Bring the pork to room temperature.

Preheat the oven to 400°F. Open out the pocket of the pork loin and pack it loosely with the stuffing, pressing toward the center so that the long edges will meet and keep the stuffing inside. Tie the roast in 4 to 5 places with kitchen twine and place it on a rack in a roasting pan. In a small saucepan, heat the remaining $1/4$ cup sherry, mustard, and marmalade just to the simmering point, whisking. Brush the mixture evenly over the roast. Place in the oven and roast for 10 minutes, then reduce the heat to 325°F and cook for a total time (including the first 10 minutes) of about 23 minutes per pound, basting occasionally with the sherry mixture. When the temperature at the thickest part of the meat (not the stuffing) reaches 165°F, the roast is done. Timing will depend on the thickness of the roast. Rest the pork, loosely covered with foil, for 10 to 15 minutes, then slice $1/2$- to $3/4$-inch thick. Serve on warm plates.

# Duck Sausage Tacos with Mango Salsa

SERVES 4

I prefer soft tacos because there is no need to set up the deep fryer and they are much lower in fat than crisp tacos. Or, you could make these into tostadas simply by shallow-frying the tortillas until crisp and then mounding all the ingredients on top, using the crisped tortilla like a plate.

For a shortcut, use a good store-bought salsa, preferably fruit-based. Have everyone standing around the kitchen while you prepare these simple roll-ups, because they are truly a "pan-to-mouth" food.

## Mango Salsa:

1 ripe mango, peeled, pitted, and cut into $1/4$-inch dice
4 green onions, white and light green parts only, thinly sliced on the diagonal
4 ripe strawberries, cut into $1/4$-inch dice
$1/4$ cup finely chopped fresh cilantro leaves
1 jalapeño chile, or to taste, stemmed, seeded, and finely diced
2 tablespoons fresh lime juice
$1/2$ teaspoon sea salt

3 links (about $3/4$ pound total) fresh, reduced-fat, mild duck sausages, such as Jody Maroni's All-Duck with Fennel, Coriander, & Sage, casings removed
8 small flour tortillas, wrapped in a towel and warmed in a low oven
1 cup shredded iceberg lettuce
$1/4$ cup finely diced white onion

In a glass or ceramic bowl, combine the mango, green onions, strawberries, cilantro, chile, lime juice, and salt. Toss together gently to mix, cover and refrigerate for up to 2 hours before serving.

Heat a large nonstick or cast-iron skillet over medium heat. Add the sausage and cook, crumbling and separating the meat with a wooden spoon, until only just cooked through, about 6 minutes. Do not overcook or the sausage meat will be dry. With a slotted spoon, transfer the sausage meat to a double layer of paper towels to drain briefly.

Mound some of the sausage in the center of each warmed tortilla. Top with an even layer of lettuce and a sprinkling of the onion. Top with a tablespoon or two of the Mango Salsa, roll up loosely and serve at once.

# Cabbage Leaves Stuffed with Lamb Sausage, Wild Mushrooms, and Apples

**SERVES 6**

This is a slightly unorthodox take on a dish that has been keeping Eastern Europeans and other cold-weather denizens satisfied for generations. I like the freshness of apple in the stuffing, and the contrasting earthiness of wild mushrooms. The addition of mint lifts the flavor to a bright, fresh level that is anything but old-fashioned. Of course, you could substitute any fresh, reduced-fat sausage for the lamb sausage: Jody Maroni's Pork Apple-Maple Sausage makes a nice variation, in which case I'd suggest adding 2 teaspoons of Dijon-style mustard to the stuffing.

1 large head Savoy cabbage, damaged outer leaves removed
4 links (about 1 pound total) fresh, reduced-fat lamb sausage, such as Jody Maroni's Moroccan Sausage with Tangerines, Wine, & Currants, casings removed
$1/2$ cup dried porcini mushrooms, soaked for 20 minutes in very hot water
1 tablespoon butter
1 tablespoon vegetable oil
$1/2$ medium-size onion, finely chopped
2 Granny Smith apples, peeled, cored, and cut into $1/2$-inch chunks
1 teaspoon chopped fresh sage or $1/2$ teaspoon dried sage, crumbled
$1/2$ teaspoon sea salt
Freshly ground black pepper, to taste
1 tablespoon chopped fresh parsley
1 tablespoon, plus 1 teaspoon chopped fresh mint
$1/2$ cup dry white wine, low-fat, low-sodium chicken broth, or water

Carefully remove 8 of the largest outer leaves of the cabbage, keeping them as intact as possible. Remove 2 or 3 more leaves to use for patching, and reserve the remaining cabbage for another use. Trim the tough white base away from each leaf and bring a very large pot of generously salted water to the boil. Blanch the leaves in 2 batches for 5 to 6 minutes, or until tender and pliable but still bright green. Drain quickly and, to preserve their color, plunge into a bowl of ice water. Gently spread the leaves out on tea towels while you make the filling.

Steam the sausages for 15 minutes over simmering water. Drain briefly on paper towels, slice $1/2$-inch thick on the diagonal, and cut the slices crosswise in half. Place in a large bowl.

Squeeze the mushrooms as dry as possible and chop coarsely. In a large skillet, heat the butter and oil over medium-low heat. Add the onion and cook for about 5 minutes, stirring, until tender. Add the mushrooms, apples, sage, salt, and pepper. Cover and cook for about 8 minutes, stirring occasionally, until the apples have softened. Stir in the parsley and 1 tablespoon of the mint and add to the bowl with the sausages. Toss together well.

Preheat the oven to 375°F. Lightly oil a large covered casserole.

Place a cabbage leaf with the stem end facing you on the work surface. Spoon about $1/2$ cup of the filling at the base of the leaf. Roll up, tucking in the sides, to make a firm package and place seam-side down in the casserole. Repeat with the remaining leaves, making 8 large rolls and using the extra leaves to patch around the base as necessary to enclose the filling completely. Drizzle the wine over and around the rolls, cover the dish snugly with foil and bake in the oven for 45 minutes. Scatter each roll with a little mint and serve at once, drizzled with a little of the pan juices.

# Simple Cassoulet

SERVES 8 TO 10

Cassoulet is a regional French countryside dish that inspires great controversy in all who claim to have the best, the original, the *only* recipe. In fact, like the Gratin Dauphinoise on page 25, the French have been known to come to blows on the subject of which recipe is truly "authentic." I can only remind you that food is to the French as cars, or perhaps sports are to many Americans (always the top subject of conversation at any gathering). I won't claim authenticity for this recipe, but then it doesn't take 3 days to prepare, either. Using leg of lamb for this dish is expensive but makes for a lighter dish—shoulder is less expensive but a bit fattier, giving a result more like the traditional cassoulet.

2 pounds small dried white beans, such as Great Northern
1 large onion, peeled but left whole
15 medium, peeled garlic cloves, 5 left whole and 10 finely chopped
2 bay leaves
1 sprig fresh thyme
Sea salt and freshly ground black pepper
1 tablespoon vegetable oil
2 pounds boneless lamb leg or shoulder, cut into 1-inch cubes
1 onion, coarsely chopped
2 ribs celery, thinly sliced
1/3 cup tomato paste
1/2 cup dry red or white wine
4 links (about 1 pound total) fresh, reduced fat garlic pork sausage, such as Jody Maroni's Toulouse Garlic
4 links (about 1 pound total) fresh, reduced-fat fruit-flavored poultry sausage, such as Jody Maroni's Orange Garlic Cumin
4 links (about 1 pound total) fresh, reduced-fat Andouille-style sausage, such as Jody Maroni's Andouille
1 tablespoon chopped fresh thyme or 1 teaspoon dried thyme, crumbled
1/2 cup dry red wine, such as cabernet sauvignon or merlot
2 cups coarse dried bread crumbs
1/2 cup chopped fresh parsley

In a large saucepan, cover the beans with cold water and bring to a boil. Simmer for 2 minutes, then remove from the heat, cover, and let stand for 1 hour. Add the whole onion, whole garlic cloves, bay leaves, and sprig of thyme. Bring the mixture to a slow simmer and cook, covered, for 1 to 2 hours, until the beans are just tender (the cooking time will depend on the age of the beans). About halfway through the cooking time, add 1 tablespoon of salt.

While the beans cook, heat the oil in a large nonstick or cast-iron skillet. Over high heat, brown the lamb cubes until golden, turning with tongs and sprinkling with salt and pepper at the end of the cooking time. Set the lamb aside on a plate. Add the chopped onion to the skillet and cook over medium heat for 5 minutes, until translucent. Add the celery and tomato paste and cook for 3 minutes more, then add the wine and simmer until reduced by about half. Combine with the lamb.

In a large steamer or in batches, steam the sausages over simmering water for 8 minutes.

Drain briefly on paper towels and cut half of the sausages into 2-inch lengths, leaving the remaining sausages whole.

Drain the beans, reserving the liquid, and discard the onion, bay leaves, and thyme sprig. In a small bowl, combine the chopped garlic, thyme, and a pinch of pepper.

Preheat the oven to 325°F. In a large, deep casserole (cast iron and enamel is ideal) spoon a third of the beans. Nestle half the lamb and vegetable mixture and half the sausages into the beans. Scatter over half of the garlic-thyme mixture. Repeat, layering the ingredients, and cover with a third and final layer of beans. Pour in the reserved bean cooking liquid and the wine. If necessary, add enough water to almost but not quite cover the beans. Cover the pan with the lid or aluminum foil and bake for 1 hour. (At this point you could refrigerate the dish overnight or for up to 24 hours before finishing. Just give it 20 minutes at room temperature before placing in the oven.)

In a small bowl, toss the bread crumbs and parsley together. Remove the cover from the pan and spread half of the crumbs over the top. Bake uncovered for 1 hour more. Remove from the oven and gently press the crust down into the beans so that the liquid wells up over the spoon. Scatter the remaining crumb mixture over the top, increase the heat to 375°F, and return to the oven for 45 minutes longer. Allow the cassoulet to rest for about 5 minutes, then serve, giving each diner part of the top crust.

# Jody Maroni's Sausage Flavors

(All made without nitrates, preservatives, or MSG*)

### Poultry:
Yucatan Chicken & Duck Sausage with Cilantro & Beer
Orange-Garlic-Cumin Chicken & Duck Sausage with Oranges & Fresh Orange Juice
Chinese Chicken & Duck Sausage with Cashews & Sesame
Boudin Blanc Chicken & Duck Sausage with Shallots & Tarragon
All-Chicken Italian with Oranges & Wine
All-Chicken Bistro with Roasted Garlic, Rosemary, & Glacé de Canard
All-Duck with Fennel, Coriander, & Sage
Chicken & Turkey Chorizo with Fresh Mint & Balsamic Vinegar
Chicken Apple with Sherry
Chicken & Duck with Basil, Sun-dried Tomatoes, & Parmesan
Smoked Chicken Andouille

### Pork:
(many of the pork sausages are now made in poultry versions)
Hot Italian with Oranges, Wines, & Cheeses
Sweet Italian with Oranges, Wines, & Cheeses
Breakfast Sausage with Buttermilk
Maple Breakfast with Pork, Bacon, & Maple Syrup
Fresh Chorizo with Beer
Toulouse Garlic Sausage with Wine
Apple Maple
Bratwurst
Sausage with Figs, Marsala Wine, & Pine Nuts
Pumante Sausage with Pork, Sun-dried Tomatoes, Prosciutto, Wine, & Pine Nuts

### Pork and Beef:
Danziger Fresh Polish Sausage with Onions, Beer, & Smoke Flavor
Louisiana Boudin Hot Links with Rice, Green Onions, & Plenty of Spices

### Lamb and Pork:
Bombay Curried Sausage with Monoucka Raisins
Moroccan Sausage with Tangerines, Wine, & Currants

* The smoked sausage(s) contain nitrates

### 1 (800) HAUTDOG

*91*

# Making
# Your
# Own sausages

# Making Your Own

There are several ways to make sausage at home, ranging from the high-tech (a $95 meat grinder and $300 stuffer available from The Sausage Maker in Buffalo, NY, see page 94) to the low-tech (two good knives and a wide-mouthed funnel). The supremely important constant of any method, whether you choose to put your sausage in some kind of casing or simply form it into patties, is hygiene. All equipment and work surfaces used for making sausage must be scrupulously clean, and both the ingredients and equipment must be chilled prior to sausagemaking to prevent the temperature from reaching the level at which bacteria become active. There are some wonderful books which treat the subject of sausagemaking exhaustively, such as *The Complete Sausage Cookbook*, by Jack Sleight, and *Great Sausage Recipes and Meat Curing*, by Rytek Kutas (there's a video, too). If you plan to make sausagemaking your summer or winter project and anticipate purchasing specialized equipment, we recommend that you track down one of these books to ensure success at what can become a costly hobby. For the novice, however, we include the simple recipe below to start you off. Of course, with the proliferation of reduced-fat and exotic-flavored sausages coming to the market, it may be easier to drive to the butcher or supermarket. If your area is not well served or you want the very best, **order Jody Maroni Sausages by air at 1 (800) HAUTDOG, or visit the website at www.maroni.com.**

One extra bonus of making your own sausage is that you can make them extremely low in fat. Sausages which are produced on a larger scale, even by today's artisanal companies like Jody Maroni's, must have some fat added to keep them moist during transport and holding in restaurants before serving. In this recipe, there is no *added* fat at all, so each sausage contains only about 4 grams of fat. Remember to keep the cooking time brief (see page 11), because a sausage this lean can dry out quickly if overcooked. But don't think this sausage is any less flavorful because it's extra lean! You still have that wonderful burst of juices and aroma when you cut into this light and summery 'wurst,' flecked with bright red pepper and tiny hints of green from the green onions. There is something intensely satisfying about making your own sausage. Try it and see—you might just get hooked!

## Homemade Chicken Sausage

MAKES 1 3/4 POUNDS

Chopping meat for sausage can be accomplished either with a sharp cleaver or chef's knife, or in a meat grinder (brief freezing makes chopping the chicken much easier). Good quality stand mixers have optional food grinders and sausage stuffing attachments with fairly good instructions included, but see the book references above for more detailed instructions. If using a stand mixer, make absolutely sure the shaft fits firmly and securely into the socket, so it will turn evenly and force the sausage mixture into the casings.

Using a food processor for chopping meat tends to crush rather than chop, giving a mushy texture without definition, so I don't recommend it.

Again, it is imperative that all the ingredients and equipment you will be using are well chilled.

Natural hog casings (see note, optional)
1 3/4 pounds boneless, skinless chicken thigh meat
1/2 cup finely diced red bell pepper (about 1/2 medium pepper)
3 green onions, both green and white part, finely chopped (or substitute 1/3 cup chopped chives, cilantro, or parsley)
1/2 cup corn kernels (if frozen, thawed and drained well)
3 garlic cloves, very finely chopped
1/4 cup beer or distilled water
1 teaspoon tequila or rum (optional)
1 3/4 teaspoons sea salt
1/2 teaspoon ground white pepper
1/2 teaspoon ground black pepper
1/2 teaspoon ground cumin
1/2 teaspoon ground ginger
Pinch ground coriander
Pinch crushed red pepper flakes, or to taste

*Continued over*

Prepare all the vegetables and assemble all the spices before you begin.

If you will be stuffing the sausage into casings: place the casings in a large bowl in the kitchen sink. Fit one end of the casing over the kitchen tap and run water gently through it so it swirls and rinses the inside and outside evenly. Find the ends of each intact length of casing and continue rinsing until you think you have enough for your batch. You will need about 4 feet for this recipe (about 2 feet per pound of sausage mixture is the general rule). Let the casings soak in plenty of cold water for about 30 minutes.

Cut the chicken meat into 1-inch chunks and place in one layer on a tray which will fit inside your freezer. Freeze for 10 minutes.

Either, **A.**) With a sharp cleaver, cut the chunks into long, thin strips, then slice crosswise into $1/8$- to $1/4$-inch dice, or **B.**) put the chunks of chicken through the $1/4$-inch plate of a meat grinder.

In a large, chilled mixing bowl, combine the chopped chicken, red pepper, green onions, corn, garlic, beer, tequila, if using, and seasonings. Mix together quickly but thoroughly, distributing all the colorful ingredients evenly (but do not over-mix; the mixture must stay as cold as possible).

If using casings, use the sausage stuffing attachment of your mixer, a wide-mouthed sausage funnel, a large piping bag fitted with a plain nozzle, or a sausage gun to force the mixture into the casings. Thread about 2 feet of the casing over the nozzle, gently forcing it almost to the end but leaving 2 inches at the end so you can tie it off firmly (otherwise, if you tie off the end first and *then* start filling the casing, you will have a large air bubble at the end). Fill the casings in whatever method you have chosen, then pinch and twist off into links as desired, twisting each one in the same direction (or, you could leave the sausage in one long coil, which makes a beautiful presentation in dishes such as Paella, page 85). When you come to a hole in the casing, or the sausage is long enough for your liking, gently squeeze any air bubbles to the open end, then tie off securely and thread more casing over the nozzle as necessary. The sausage should not be so tight that it will burst easily, but it should be fairly firm and well filled.

If not using casings, mold the mixture into patties by hand, making 7 to 8 patties from this quantity, and place on a plate.

Refrigerate, tightly wrapped for up to 3 days, or freeze for up to one month before using.

Note: Natural hog casings (32 to 35mm) are sold packed in salt and will keep almost indefinitely in the refrigerator, which is handy since it is difficult to buy them in small quantities.

You can order them from:

The Sausage Maker
26 Military Road
Buffalo, NY 14207-2875
Tel: (716) 876-5521
Fax: (716) 875-0302

or special order from your local and/or specialty butcher. One pound of casings will make from 20 to 25 pounds of sausage. Some casings will have holes in them and must be discarded.

# index

Artichoke, fontina, and garlic sausage calzone, 77
Beans:
    black, with lime and chipotle, 33
    Portuguese stew with chicken and turkey chorizo, 80
    simple cassoulet, 90-91
Beer with sausage, 18
Black beans with lime and chipotle, 33
Boudin Blanc, raw mushroom salad with, lemon, and herbs, 63
Cabbage leaves stuffed with lamb sausage, wild mushrooms, and apples, 89
Calzone, artichoke, fontina, and garlic sausage, 77
Capellini with oysters, white wine, spicy sausage, and watercress, 72
Cassoulet, simple, 90-91
Chard and sausage sauce, 70
Chicken sausage:
    choucroute garnie with garlic and, 81
    dumpling and slippery noodle soup, 60
    homemade, 93-94
    Italian, penne with oven-roasted tomatoes, Swiss chard and, 70
    salad Niçoise with, bistro 62
    zucchini, and pasta frittata, 55
Chorizo, chicken and turkey, Portuguese bean stew with, 80
Choucroute garnie with garlic and chicken bistro sausages, 81
Corn:
    grilled, relish, 43-44
    Toulouse garlic sausage with watercress, bruschetta and, 61
    and Yucatan sausage soufflé, 56
Couscous with red and yellow tomatoes, 35
Curry mayonnaise, 67
Dolmades with yogurt sauce, 51
Duck sausage:
    jambalaya, 83
    little pizzas with fennel and smoked mozzarella, 73
    paella with shrimp and, 85-86
    tacos with mango salsa, 88
Dumplings, chicken sausage, and slippery noodle soup, 60
Eggs:
    huevos a la flamenco, 57
    chicken sausage, zucchini, and pasta frittata, 55
    corn and Yucatan sausage soufflé, 56
Eggplant and garlic sausage sandwich with curry mayonnaise, 67
Fig, marsala, and pine nut sausage stuffing with roasted pork loin, 87
French potato salad, 24
Frittata, chicken sausage, zucchini, and pasta, 55
Fusilli with wine-braised sausage and carrots, 71
Garlic sausage:
    artichoke and fontina calzone, 77

choucroute garnie with chicken bistro and, 81
and eggplant sandwich with curry mayonnaise, 67
and rosemary ravioli, 49-50
salad with corn, watercress, and bruschetta, 61
Goat cheese:
    grilled sausage salad with dandelion greens and, 65
    phyllo triangles with spinach, lamb sausage and, 52
    and sausage purses, 53-54
Gratin dauphinoise, 25
Grilled corn relish, 43-44
Grilled sausage salad with dandelion greens and fresh goat cheese, 65
Grilled skewers of sausage, apples, bay leaves, and country bread, 82
Horseradish dill potato salad, 23
Huevos a la flamenco, 57
Jambalaya, duck sausage, 83
Lamb sausage:
    cabbage leaves stuffed with wild mushrooms, apples and, 89
    phyllo triangles with spinach, feta and, 52
Leftover sausage, 67
Lentils, warm, with mustard dressing, 31-32
Mango salsa, duck sausage tacos with, 88
Mushrooms:
    salad with boudin blanc, lemon, and herbs, 63
    soft polenta with Parmesan and, 34
    wild, cabbage leaves stuffed with lamb sausage, apples and, 89
Mustard dressing, warm lentils with, 31-32
New Orleans oyster and sausage po'boy, 66
Niçoise salad, with chicken bistro sausage, 62
Noodle and chicken sausage dumpling soup, 60
Oven-roasted tomatoes, penne with chicken-Italian sausage, Swiss chard and, 70
Oyster and sausage po'boy, New Orleans, 66
Oysters, white wine, spicy sausage, and watercress, capellini with, 72
Paella with duck sausage and shrimp, 85-86
Pasta, chicken sausage, and zucchini frittata, 55
Penne with chicken-Italian sausage, oven-roasted tomatoes, and Swiss chard, 70
Persian rice pilaf, 36
Phyllo triangles with spinach, lamb sausage, and feta, 52
Pickled shallots, 41
Pizzas:
    little duck sausage, with fennel and smoked mozzarella, 73
    rustica, 75-76
Polenta, soft, with mushrooms and Parmesan, 34
Pork loin, roasted, with fig, marsala, and pine nut sausage stuffing, 87
Portuguese bean stew with chicken and turkey

chorizo, 80
Potato(es):
    French salad, 24
    gratin dauphinoise, 25
    horseradish dill salad, 23
    roasted, with chipotle and cilantro, 22
Precooking sausage, 14
Ravioli, garlic sausage and rosemary, 49-50
Relish, grilled corn, 43-44
Rice pilaf, Persian, 36
Salsa cruda, 40
Salsa, mango, duck sausage tacos with, 88
Sandwiches:
    eggplant and garlic sausage with curry mayonnaise, 67
    Jody Maroni sausage, 19
    New Orleans oyster and sausage po'boy, 66
Sausage(s):
    capellini with oysters, white wine, watercress and, 72
    cooking tips, 14, 16-17
    flavors of, Jody Maroni, 91
    and fresh goat cheese purses, 53-54
    grilled, salad with dandelion greens and fresh goat cheese, 65
    grilled skewers of apples, bay leaves, country bread and, 82
    grilling tips, 14
    homemade, 93-94
    leftover, 67
    lower-fat, 11
    and oyster po'boy, New Orleans, 66
    precooking, 14
    red wine-braised, fusilli with carrots and, 71
    sandwich, Jody Maroni, 19
    *see also specific types*
Shallots, pickled, 41
Soufflé, corn and Yucatan sausage, 56
Soup, chicken sausage dumpling and slippery noodle, 60
Spinach, lamb sausage, and feta, phyllo triangles with, 52
Stew, Portuguese bean with chicken and turkey chorizo, 80
Stuffing, roasted pork loin with fig, marsala, and pine nut sausage, 87
Tacos, duck sausage, with mango salsa, 88
Tomatoes:
    oven-roasted, penne with chicken-Italian sausage, Swiss chard and, 70
    red and yellow, couscous with, 35
Toulouse garlic sausage salad with corn, watercress, and bruschetta, 61
Yogurt sauce, dolmades with, 51
Yucatan sausage and corn soufflé, 56